A NEW PARADIGM OF DEVELOPMENT
Sumangalam

A NEW PARADIGM OF DEVELOPMENT

Sumangalam

Bajrang Lal Gupta

GYAN

A New Paradigm of Development: Sumangalam

Rs. 540

ISBN: 978-81-212-1059-1

Published in 2010 in India by
Gyan Publishing House
23, Main Ansari Road, Daryaganj,
New Delhi - 110002
Phone : 23282060, 23261060
Fax : (011) 23285914
e-mail : books@gyanbooks.com
gyanbook@vsnl.com

website : gyanbooks.com

Laser Type Setting by: Rudra Computer Graphics, Delhi
Printed at : Gian Ridhi Offset Printers, Delhi

Contents

Foreword

(Sarvatobhadra Sumangalam)

Development has become a catchphrase of modernity but it has been narrowly identified with material development alone. A discourse on social welfare has been initiated although it is still on the fringes. Our idea of development is seriously flawed by the belief that that we have risen to a state of quasi-development from being underdeveloped and now moving towards full development. This erroneous outlook stems from the fact that we have adopted 'development theory' as gospel truth. We dare not rethink the adopted paradigm because modern science and the entire social thinking are so deeply influenced by this theory. Even if we assume the 'struggle for existence' and 'survival of the fittest' to be truisms and facts of nature, do they still qualify to be the standards of our civilizations? These could not be our ideals even if they were facts of life. Then there is no question of dichotomy between the desired (Preya) and beneficial (Shreya), and there is no place for industriousness and morality in this automatic or natural order of things. But history is witness that cooperation and not competition is the rock of human development. Even today the tribesmen and forest dwellers are lively and peace-loving because there is cooperation and self-reliance in an environment of simplicity.

It is for this reason that Indian worldview ordains 'four labours' (purushasthas) for true development which is integral and universal. The 'four labours' (Chaturpurusharthas) includes not only Artha (material objects) but also Kama (Pleasure seeking) and both are founded on Dharma (Eternal Law). Material pursuits and indulgence in pleasure may be associated with life but the goal of life is Moksha (Spiritual Salvation). This salvation is the acme of our development. Despite dog-eat-dog state or 'struggle for existence'-the harmony of 'four labours' is outlined in the concept of 'five sheaths' (physical, vital, mental, intelligence and bliss) which is an indication towards unity. Though accepting the importance of matter in life, we find the material interpretation of history as incomplete and lopsided. To attain a state of true development and civilization without concomitant moral and spiritual development is a mirage. To have the pleasant without the beneficial, science without spirituality and mechanization without humanism will prove ruinous for us.

It is for this reason that invocation of 'let all be happy' have been the cornerstone of our worldview. Mahatma Gandhi's 'Sarvodaya' (emancipation for all) might be an innovation, but this is the signature tune of Indian thought. This view has been nourished by the tradition of saints like Kabir, Tulsi and Surdas to Gandhi-Vinoba Bhave. Almost 2500 years ago, Jain savant Samantbhadra's "Yuktaanushana" (Integral Discipline) we find the mention of 'Sarvodaya Tirtha' (Pilgrimage for redemption of all).

Lord Buddha's 'Bahujana Hitay, Bahujan Sukhay' (for the good of everybody, for happiness of everybody) was not merely quantitative but qualitative as well. In the Dhammapada there is chapter on affection (Piyabhagga) there is a chapter on perfected one (Arahatavagga). Our ideal is nothing else but 'let every element be happy' and 'let every being be painless'. In modern times Sri Aurobindo's Supramental evolution theory is a bridge between the biological evolutionists denying the spirit and spiritualitists denying materialism. Gurudev Rabindranath Tagore was a devotee of 'Satyam, Shivam, Sundaram' or Truth is Divine, and Divine is Beautiful. Founding of Sri Niketan alongside Shanti Niketan is its proof. The 'Integral Humanism' of Pt. Deendayal Upadhyaya is an effective expression of this philosophy. The 'Sarvodaya' was no Utopia, and is founded by 'Antyodaya' (emancipation of the lowliest) which was Gandhi's mantra.

This is also the substance of Dr. Lohia's Seven Revolutions or Jai Prakash Narain's Total Revolution. The development of all in all manners can alone be acknowledged as development.

But this spiritual state has to be realized at social and organizational levels through the Vedic ideal

"Vishwapustam Grame asmin Anaaturam' (A world nourished by villages). For this we have to re-experiment with Acharya Vinobha's gift of village (Gram Daan) and Gram Swaraj. We accept neither capitalist privatization nor state ownership of Communist rule. We have to achieve village-centric model.

Consequent upon the Battle of Plassey, 1757 India was turned into a colony by the British. They not only drained India economically but enslaved as culturally. The British considered India as a colony. Dadabhai Nauroji has expounded upon this exploitation in his landmark book Poverty and Un-British Rule in India. The Macualay's charter of enslavement alienated Indians from Indianess.

In India Greeks, Sakas, Scythians, Pathan and Mughal etc came. But until the self-sufficient and self-reliant villages remained, Indian culture remained safe. This was our Swarajya, our cultural sovereignty. On August 15, 1947 we got political independence but the agenda of Swarajya remains unfinished. Globalization and 'Special Economic Zone' is a demon that is going to lay waste of our village system and village culture in a planned manner. This will end our sovereignty by creating 'state within state'. It would enslave India to new neo-imperialism like the East India Company accomplished once. The sovereignty of the village, agriculture of the village, labour of the village, development of the village, assembly of the village, treasury of the village, guards of the villages, school of the village – this is India's true Gram Swaraj.

The writer has diagnosed the Descartes' Mind-body dichotomy and dualism, and Newton's scientific rationalism to be at the root of the crisis of Western civilization. To my mind, the Cartesian and Newtonian theories of duality the philosophy of life built on Darwin's evolution theory has proved more detrimental than. It ruptured the unity of creation and human society leading to the propagation of a distorted social philosophy. There is more cooperation and amity between nature and humanity than there is struggle between them. Darwin's fundamental postulation that there is struggle between environment and organism and between organisms and organisms has been overplayed.

This philosophy was behind the Marxian theory of class conflict. My contention is that the struggle for survival, whether fully true or partly, could not be a civilized philosophy of life. Otherwise the old people and children, ill and the infirm should not be alive on earth. Let alone human society, the instrincts of sacrifice, motherliness etc are to be found in animal society as well. The history of human society is full of love, unselfishness, altruism. There is a difference between humanliness and animalness.

The Indian view of life has refused to recognize the duality between matter and spirit. It is quite evident in the Upanishadic notion of 'five sheaths' (Panch Koshas). In modern time also, Sri Aurobindo tried to end the isolation of materialism and spirituality. Swami Vivekananda said to the extent that food should precede metaphysics.

Spirituality is vacuity without materialism and materialism is blind incompleteness without spirituality. Modern science is abolishing the division between matter and consciousness. Sir James Jeans has long ago brought to light the fundamental unity between matter and elements of consciousness; whereas Max Plank, Heisenberg highlighted the inseparability of matter and spirit. The entire universe is dynamic and conscious. Whether we call it cosmos or universal Self, matter or Consciousness, in reality all is an interplay of dynamic sentient subatomic partlices. The entire universe is its expression.

However, we do not wish to lose ourselves in this ethereal thoughts but contemplate upon the problems of life. Unfortunately, the social aspect of the Indian society did not develop in proportion to its spiritual aspect. It is for this reason that split apart by invasions we had to remain in servitude for nearly thousand years. Our division of four labours, knowledge of 7000 species in biological world, our Gurukul system of education, Panchayati system all were eclipsed and substituted by superstition and ritualism.

We believe that manliness of India will rise again as in 1857, or 1942 or at least a 1974 will happen. Deathless transition of epoch is our heritage; it is our destiny as well. We are children of immortality, we will not perish. A perennial, harmonious and comprehensive development of all is our goal.

The current book is a resounding declaration of Gram Swaraj at a time coinciding with the centenary of Hind Swaraj. It can become the charter of India's existance and temporal development as well. I find not merely in agreement with his views, but a better presentation of my own belief. The book affords an alternative vision in the age of globalization and liberalization. It has a remarkable potential for generating discourse on economic question, and play a central role on policy formulation and implementation.

The author of this book is awakening us as a priest. We compliment and hail him.

Dr. Ramjee Singh
Former Vice Chancellor. Jain
Vishwa Bharati Vishwavidyalaya,
Ladanne (Rajasthan),
Former Secretary, Afro-Asian
Philosophical Association,
Founder Head, Department of
Gandhiyan Thought
Bhagalpur University (Bihar),
Ex-Member of Parliament.

Introduction

The concept of development has remained a widely debated subject during the last one hundred years. This period has witnessed different phases of development struggle and also of the varieties of perceptions, approaches and frameworks of development paradigms that have been put forward by the various eminent scholars and expert groups. According to Meier and Rauch (Leading Issues in Economic Development, Preface, XV) the economics of development is one of the most exciting as well as a frustrating subject in social sciences. Now we have with us a long sequence of experiences of various approaches, policies, systems and development models but all of them are proving inadequate in solving the problems of mankind at large. Instead of solving the problems, the development models are actually creating and aggravating problems. We can see that poverty, inequality and unemployment are increasing all over the world. Environmental degradation, increase in pollution levels, phenomenon of global warming and climatic changes are virtually threatening the very existence of the globe. Decline in ethical, cultural and human values and degradation of the family and community life have made the things much worse. Seeing all these things people are forced to think whether we are heading towards destruction in pursuit of development? Thus we find today, the world economy, and in particular, the developing world is at a crossroads in its development struggle.

It seems our late President and great philosopher Dr. S. Radhakrisnhan is right in the contemporary context also when he says, "Men of intelligence and enterprise are convinced that there is something radically wrong with the arrangements and institutions in regard to politics, economics and industry and that we must get rid of them if we are to serve humanity" (Radhakrisnhan, Religion and Society). Now all knowledgeable persons of the world are struggling to figure a new approach and system. For the last several years a number of questions have been cropping up in my mind also in regard to the concept, meaning, measurement, approach and direction of development. From this emerges a question, can the perusal and study of the Bharatiya values and way of life provide us the guidelines for the future course of actions and policies in the field of development?

On this note, I started my journey in search of a new paradigm of development. In this process, I tried to present my views through seminars, symposia and lectures at several places. Since then many of my friends have suggested me to present my views in the form of a book. Fortunately, in March 2007, Madhav Smriti Nyas, Ahmedabad invited me to deliver three lectures on this topic. Truly speaking, the present book took shape from these lectures.

A synoptic view of some of the dilemmas and paradoxes of the development model is discussed in the book. It analyses development within the context of a major set of problems, such as poverty, inequality, unemployment, environmental decay, moral and social degradation, and rural stagnation. It adopts a problem- and policy-oriented approach to the development economics. It recognizes the necessity of the treating the problems of development and underdevelopment from an institutional and structural (non-economic) as well as an economic perspective. It thus attempts to combine relevant theory with realistic institutional analyses. It considers the many economic, social and institutional problems of underdevelopment as closely inter-related and requiring simultaneous and coordinated holistic approach to their solution. After elaborating the problems and inconsistencies of present western development model, I made a humble attempt to present a new paradigm of development basically based on Bharatiya values of life and named it as the concept of "Sumangalam". It is a holistic and integral approach of development and encompasses a very wide range of issues. I admit that it is practically impossible to elaborate them all in the limited pages of a book. My objective here is to raise issues, initiate a dialogue, debate and discussion, and intervene in the ongoing development debate by presenting my own vision of development. I therefore earnestly request to all thinkers, intellectuals, policy makers and social activists to enrich this dialogue by giving their valuable suggestions and comments on the theme. I believe that this dialogue will definitely be able to give shape to a new kind of development paradigm which will be useful not only for India but for the whole of the world.

The book has been thematically divided into three chapters. Chapter One explains the meaning and measures of western development model and its inconsistencies. Chapter Two elaborates the search for a new development path – "Sumangalam", its meaning and broad objectives. Chapter Three presents a mangal draft for socio-technical-economic structure to achieve the goals of Sumangalam and to realise it.

I express my deep gratitude to renowned Gandhian thinker Prof. Ramjee Singh who has blessed me by writing the Foreword to the book, which itself has given a higher utility-scale to my work. I am thankful to all friends who have encouraged and to some extent rather forced me to bring out this book in English and provided all sorts of help in this endeavour. Thanks are due to the staff of India Policy Foundation.

I also owe my gratitude to all scholars and eminent persons whose works have been extensively used in writing the present book. I am also thankful to Gyan Publishing House for publishing and bring out the book with quality printing and attractive getup.

Bajrang Lal Gupta
C-30, Ahinsa Vihar,
Sector - 9, Rohini,
Delhi - 110085

1

Western Development Model : Meaning, Measures and its Inconsistencies

It is evident from the present state of India that the post–Independent governmental policies and approaches have brought the Indian economy to a deep and serious trouble. Now the question is: how can we come out of this quagmire? Or, which path should India adopt for her development? There are two views in regard to the solution of this problem. According to one viewpoint India can overcome this problem with the help of alien capitalists, MNCs and international credit institutions, by adopting Western development models, techniques and technologies. Contrary to it, the second viewpoint suggests that India can acquire the capacity for its development through *Swadeshi* mechanism, technique and technology based on integrated-balanced development philosophy. These are two development paths, which have fundamental differences with regard to their directions and worldviews. Therefore, choosing either of these two models, should be broad-based and through debate. In fact, it should have been discussed at the time of Independence itself. But unfortunately, at that time we could not make any substantial effort in this direction.

During the struggle for Independence, Mahatma Gandhi and some of his associates tried to initiate a discussion and offered some important guidelines in his book entitled *Hind Swaraj*. But those who took over the reins after 1947 gave it up as useless. Perhaps, it was due to the inherent defeatist tendency that our leadership did not trust that national development could be achieved through indigenous efforts, skills, capabilities and our own institutional set-up. Hence, their natural focus of attention was the mechanism and systems of the so-called developed nations and they started imposing these alien mechanisms on India. As such, the sphere of discussion of the path of development revolved around two systems prevalent in those days: capitalism and socialism. We kept on framing and implementing our policies, programmes and plans, based either on market-controlled capitalistic economy or state-operated socialist economy or a combination of the two. Now, we have the benefit of experiences of the countries, which adopted capitalistic or socialistic systems as well as the experience of India. In the light of these experiences it is the most appropriate time to start a discussion on an alternative development model.

Western Development Philosophy and Development Model

Leaving aside the question of ownership over the means of production, both the systems (i.e. capitalistic and socialistic systems) have some basic similarities with regard to the concepts of man and development, materialistic approach, techniques and technologies and the partial and fragmented view of life. That is why both the systems are facing and generating the same type of problems. Hence, we can conveniently club both the systems under a single head and call it Western model or Western approach. At present this Western development-path has been ruling all the countries of the world along with India. Therefore, it is a vital necessity to assess it well before putting forward the discussion of a new development–path.

The summary of the basic fundamentals of the Western philosophy and model is as follows-

1. Fragmented mechanistic world-view based on Cartesian-Newtonian philosophy-

The Western economic thought has stemmed from the fragmented mechanistic world-view based on the Cartesian-Newtonian philosophy. This is based on the views and observations of Galileo, Bacon, Descartes and Newton etc. The following are the main assumptions of this world-view.

(a) The whole gamut of cosmos or the nature is equivalent to a vast machine which is regulated by some definite rules and this can be studied by the means of experiments and logical analysis.

(b) There is an outer world which has a completely different identity from that of ours. Therefore, we can measure this world by way of objective analysis remaining completely outside of it.

(c) Only that can be included in the field of science which can be measured and presented in terms of mathematical formulae. It has resulted in the development of deterministic approach and different branches of science have been based on it. According to this kind of science all the realities of the universe can be construed by the techniques and the procedures of mathematical analysis. Moreover, as a result of this view, evolution of those disciplines and procedures has only taken place which measure human behaviours, human realizations, sensibilities, expectations, aspirations and emotions.

(d) Different problems can be looked and studied in different forms and components. What we believe to be the totality is indeed a summation of different parts of its own.

(e) By triumphing over the nature with the help of science, man can make use of it completely for the sake of its own benefit. And it is this which opens the path of development. It is from this thought that a kind of science has emerged which teaches the technique and technology for the maximum utilization of nature with the least labour.

It is on the basis of this approach of Newton that Jon Locke has propounded the laws that direct and regulate the human behaviour. Later on, from this emerged a socio-economic structure based on individualism, private ownership of property, free market mechanism and minimal government intervention which was called the capitalistic system. In order to uphold and sustain its own identity amidst the cut-throat competition of open market mechanism, the industrial society emerging from this kind of capitalistic system, felt the necessity of a continuous reform in a continuously enlarging market, availability of cheap labour and raw materials and technology. Out of this necessity alone the capitalistic societies had indiscriminately exploited nature and also the weaker and the resource-less people within the country. Further as a result of this, these industrialized nations suppressed and exploited Asian, African and Latin American countries on all counts by imposing their rules and now a new conspiracy of exploitation has begun in the name of development of these countries. Consequently, the social and ethical values have been rapidly lagging behind.

As a reaction to the capitalistic exploitation, Marx proposed a system of communism which was incommensurate with the open market mechanism. But Marx also used the same Cartesian-Newtonian mechanical world-view as the base of his scientific socialism. The only difference was that he vigorously opposed the exploitation of labour by the capitalists and emphasized on the nationalization of the means of production and resources. But it is because of the continuity of the mechanical world-view, the exploitation of nature and men persisted in this system also; only the place and nature of exploitation had changed.

The main shortcoming of the Western techno-economic thought is that it wants unlimited progress with the limited resources of the earth. It is only because of this reason that the situations of mad race of accumulation, plundering, imperialism, exploitation, inequality and struggling are still going on.

2. ASSUMPTIONS

The main assumptions of Western economic thought are as follows:

(i) The concept of an economic man:

The Western economics is based on the assumption of economic man and it is defined as a man whose decisions and inspirations are based on wealth or material gains. Since the main driving force behind different activities of such a man is economic considerations hence, he is called an 'Economic Man'.

The whole development theory of the West has been established assuming a man as an 'economic man'. It is worth thinking how valid this assumption is. When somebody says that this is a steam-engine, it implies that this engine works by the force of steam. Akin to this, when somebody says that this is an electric motor, it means that the motor runs by electricity. In a similar way, when the western thinkers assume a man as 'economic man', it means that the man is moved by money (*Arth*). It also implies that the only criterion for all the decisions of man is receiving or not receiving money or receiving less or more amount of money. Imagine, what benefit will the society get from a model of development which is based on such kind of the concept of economic man and what will be its consequences. On what basis will an individual, being an economic man, take decisions when he goes to the market as a consumer? He will think of buying only if the price is less and won't buy if the price is high. He will try to pay as much less as possible and in return will try to get commodities as more as possible. What will be his behaviour as a producer? He will produce that commodity which is more profitable and won't produce that which is less profitable, although it may harm the society. In this situation the production of commodities essential for the welfare of the society cannot be his priority. As a seller he will try to get the maximum amount of money in exchange for a minimum amount of commodities. He will sell to those who pay more and won't sell to those who will pay less. As an employee or a labourer he will try to get maximum remuneration by putting the least possible labour. As an employer (or owner) he will make effort to get the maximum work done by paying the minimum remuneration. On the whole, how can a society run if all the men start behaving as an economic man? How would it be possible to build up a moral society out of this? In this situation, why should one take care of parents, or where from the will of defending one's own country emerge putting his own life in stake during an assault?

(ii) Assumptions of self- interest and economic rationality:

All the Western thinkers presume that every individual works for his own interest and the individual himself can take the most appropriate decision in regard to his own interest. Since the society consists of individuals, therefore, when every individual will think of his own interest, then the interest of the society will automatically be fulfilled. According to them, the collective interest of a society is the summation of all individual interests.

The meaning of economic rationality is that an individual will be prepared to do the work where he is supposed to get the maximum benefit or the sole criterion for an individual's decision should be to get the maximum economic benefit for himself.

Anybody who behaves in accordance to this criterion is called rational in economic sense. The economic theories are constructed on the basis of this very assumption of economic rationality.

(iii) Competition and conflict are the only bases of equilibrium and progress:

This has been acknowledged in the Western economic thought that competition and conflict are going on at different levels between various economic classes and economic units. The state of equilibrium is established in an economic system as a consequence of this competition and conflict. Again the equilibrium is disturbed because of this competition and conflict and a new equilibrium is established once again.

Thus, the sequence of competition, conflict and equilibrium only determine the path and direction of development. For example, Competition amongst the buyers, also amongst the sellers and between the buyers and sellers brings the equilibrium price in the market. It is from this that the concepts such as consumers' equilibrium, producers' equilibrium, least cost combination, equilibrium with maximum profit and minimum loss etc. have emerged.

(iv) Survival of the fittest:

Being predisposed by the theory of evolution given by Darwin, the Western thinkers have also acknowledged that only that person can save and sustain his own identity amidst the competition and conflict, who can prove himself to be economically superior in comparison to others. The person who is economically feeble and frail gradually keeps on perishing. Therefore, every one tends to accumulate and demonstrate his economic potency with a view of sustaining his own identity.

(v) Nature is the maid of man:

The Western economic thinkers have accepted nature as the maid of man. They presume that the use of nature is solely for augmenting their pleasure and convenience and it is their right. Hence, with the intention of conquering nature, they have developed various methodologies, technologies and techniques in order to make utmost exploitation of it.

3. Vision and strategy regarding development

The main points of the vision and approach adopted by the Western economists in regard to development and the strategy which they have accepted for this have been given below:

(i) **Development has been defined in terms of increase in real per capita GDP**. But we know that the measurement of GDP and its calculation for the purpose of development is incomplete, faulty and flawed. An in-depth discussion on it will follow later.

(ii) **The increase in the standard of living by consuming more and more goods and services is assumed as the aim of life.**
Let's see what is meant by standard of living. How is the increase and decrease in the standard of living determined? The standard of living, to the Western thought, is determined by the basket of goods and services available with the individual for his consumption. It implies that the more the goods and services available to an individual the higher the standard of living will be. If we accept this definition, an individual will make an effort to indulge day and night in the consumption to the maximum. He will be affected by some kind of disease as a consequence of this unrestrained consumption and will have to take the help of the services of a doctor and medicines for getting rid of it. Now the amount of goods and services available with him has further increased. Hence in accordance to this definition, it has to be accepted that his standard of living has gone to a higher level. Contrary to it, if an individual has adopted restrained consumption pattern then he remains free from diseases.

Consequently, he does not require a doctor's services and medicines. Thus, he has lesser amount of goods and services, and therefore, his standard of living will be taken as lower according to this definition. Acknowledging this kind of rise in the standard of living as the aim of development may well be treated as misdirection or wrong approach. To the Western thinkers, the pace of development can be enhanced only by augmenting the level of consumption and adopting the consumeristic life style. They assume that if the consumption will increase at a higher rate, the demand will also increase. The increase in demand will lead to the increase in production which ultimately speeds up the pace of development in a country. It is for this reason that the development model of today has conceded maximum earning for maximum consumption as the central activity of an economy. But adverse consequences of it have also started coming to the limelight. Today the entire world has been victimized of the problem of consumerism. Thus, the Western thought is *artha-* and *kama-* (or earning and consumption) centered incomplete thought.

(iii) Emphasis on the increase in production to satisfy the ever-increasing desire and lust for consumption:-

When maximum consumption is taken as the aim of life, attempt is made by all means to increase the requirements of man and it is even considered good. This is the reason that the increase in wants and consumption has been seen as the rise in the level of the civilization. The society or the groups of individuals who have greater wants are considered more civilized. Thus, it becomes indispensable to increase production to fulfill these increased wants and consumptions. This is the reason that the Western thought has accepted the race of consumption and production as the path of development.

(iv) To increase production two course of actions are adopted: (a) maximum exploitation of natural resources and (b) establishment of large industrial production structure based on machine-driven and energy-consuming technology :- The natural resources are exploited to the maximum with a view to obtaining more production at the least possible time. As a consequence of it, we are gradually being the prey of the problem of environmental degradation and pollution. Big industries are being established by giant companies in order to produce at a large scale and the production is undertaken with the help of highly energy consuming plants and machines. This has brought about problems like unemployment and energy crisis.

(v) Emphasis on investment and capital–formation:- In this model capital is taken as the main factor to operate this production technique and production-structure (assuming the socio-cultural and human factors as constants). The socio-cultural and human factors are assumed constant in all the development models constructed on the basis of the Western thought. For the increase in production and development, capital is assigned the prime place by them. Therefore, increase in capital investment is acknowledged as indispensable for enhancing the pace of development. More capital accumulation for more investment is highly emphasized. Thus, the capital-intensive development strategy has been recognized. This justifies the increasing dependence of the poor countries of the world and they are taking large amount of assistance and investment from the World Bank, International Monetary Fund and the multinational companies in the name of the development. This has pushed these countries to the debt trap.

Based on the aforesaid philosophy and approach, numerous theories and models of development have come out. The Nehru-Mahalanobis model of our country is also one of them.

4. Development economics – a question mark?

Although since the days of Adam Smith views have always been expressed regarding economic development, yet the economists have paid more attention to it only after the Second World War. As we know, many countries in Asia and Africa got freedom after the Second World War. During the period of dependence, the imperialist (today's so-called developed) countries had done brutal economic exploitation of them. As a result, the economic condition of these countries was very miserable at the time of their independence. Therefore, these countries felt the necessity of their economic development after their political independence. There arose an intense feeling that political freedom has no meaning without economic development and economic progress is essential for the sustenance of their political independence also. The pressure of peoples' aspirations in the democratic system adopted by these countries also compelled the governments to speed up the endeavour for development.[1]

The increasing economic inequalities among different countries of the world also intensified the need for development-effort. Very few countries of the world would become advanced and affluent whereas a large number of nations would remain backward and poor; this situation can not last for long. As the peace is indivisible so is the progress. It means that the poverty of majority of the countries of the world may pose a threat to the prosperity of the developed countries also. Therefore, it is in the interest of the developed countries that they should take interest in the development of the poor countries and extend full cooperation to them in their development-effort. This realization also enhanced the interest of the advanced countries in the development of the poor countries. It is because of the increasing means of transport and communication and wide contacts with the developed world that the poor countries have started realizing more about their poverty compared with the rest of the world. Hence they became more conscious of poverty and seemed very anxious for doing away with it. When about two-thirds of the populations of the world are engulfed in economic backwardness and half of the population in malnutrition, it is but natural in such situation to be consternated for the economic development. It is only because of these reasons that after the Second World War the whole world has been attracted more towards the economic development and its problems. This is the only reason that the economic development probably remained one of the most discussed topics in the world since the latter part of the 20th century. A separate subject called 'Development Economics' emerged in the field of Economics resulting from the importance of the development and the issues related to it.

But since the last few years, a question mark seems to be emerging on the very existence of Development Economics itself as an independent subject. In both the fields, the academic world as well as in policy formulation, it does not deserve to be as important as it was earlier. In the decades of the fifty's and the sixty's the agreement that was taking place about the theories, models, policies and strategies of Development Economics and the enthusiasm which was being seen about the implementation of them through different development plans gradually decelerated. This is a serious question that how has this occurred without solving the problems of poverty and backwardness. Now, doubt has started arising about the direction, philosophy and approach of Development Economics itself. The whole atmosphere got flooded with a strange sense of fear and doubts on the path of development which this Development Economics presented and when the world marched ahead on it to some extent. That is why some economists are trying to warn not to go ahead on this path. There are many economists who even deny the necessity of 'Development Economics' as a separate subject, the prominent among them being Slutz, Heberler, Baur, Little, Walters etc. A big question mark also is being put on the assumption of Paroto's Optimum Theory. Justice cannot be catered to the poor and the downtrodden people of the society by any development model formulated on the basis of the assumption of this theory. Therefore, a section of the economists has started to suggest for the abolishing the subject of 'Development Economics' itself. Hirschman, in a way, had written the obituary of Development Economics in one of his articles entitled 'Rise and decline of Development Economics' (Essays in Trespassing, 1981). But there are many other economists who do not agree with Hirschman's view. For instance, in the opinion of Amartya Sen there is still much relevance in the broad policy themes that traditional development economics has emphasized. In this regard the observation of Meier and Rauch is worth mentioning. "....the task of development economists is made difficult because they must acquire a sense of the different assumptions that are most incisive for analyzing a problem within the context of a poor country. In particular, this calls for special care in identifying different institutional relations, in assessing the different quantitative importance of some variables, and in allowing some elements that are usually taken as givens-such as population, state of the arts, institutions, and supply of entrepreneurship - to become endogenous varibales in development analysis."[2] It is inferred from all these analysis that the intellectuals do not agree upon or are satisfied on the present from of Development Economics and its basic philosophy. They are now in search of a new paradigm. This is the challenge in the times to come and this is the work worth doing.

5. Meaning and measures of development - In the Midst of Controversies

There is long-drawn controversy in economics with regard to the meaning and measurement of development. Despite such a long debate, the meaning of development is not yet clear. When an economist intends to express his own views about development, he tells the meaning of development and furnishes it with some definition. But after sometime, he seems to be dissatisfied with his own definition. He feels that he is not telling what he wanted to tell or he is not reaching the place where he wanted to go. It is a strange situation that the development plans, development models, development policies and development strategies are being prepared and different kinds of activities are also going on in every country in the name of development without comprehending the meaning to development. This is similar to the situation when a man is not clear about the name and direction of that place where he is to go, but still he marches ahead. Moreover, there emerges a much stranger situation when he goes in the opposite direction from his destination. Today the same situation is taking place in the context of development.

Growth or development– dichotomy of terminology?

Economic growth or development – the economists are in utter confusion that out of these two terminologies which is to be used. In common parlance these two are normally used as synonymous concepts.

In the early economic literature also these two terms were used synonymously. It was for the first time that in 1911 Prof. Schumpeter made a distinction between these two terms in his article entitled 'Theory of Economic Development'. Since then, most of the economists have been trying to distinguish between these two concepts. According to Kindleberger, "economic growth means more output while economic development implies both more output as well as changes in the social, cultural, technical and institutional arrangements".[3] Normally economists have defined economic growth as a sustained increase in real GDP or per capita GDP of an economy.[4] In regard to economic developemnt we find two approaches: traditional approach and modern approach. According to traditional approach economic development implies growth plus structural change which refers to changes in technological and institutional factors. Here it is worth mentioning that in the traditional approach casual references were made with regard to the objectives of poverty elimination, economic inequalities reduction and employment generation and it is assumed that the increase in GNP or per capita GNP would automatically trickle down to the poor and unemployed.[5] However, due to the failure of traditional strategies of development in solving the problems of poverty, unemployement and inequality, it was realised that the concept of development should be redefined. Professor Dudley Seers defines the economic developement according to the new perception in the following words. "the questions to ask about a country's development are therefore : what has been happening to poverty? what has been happening to unemployment? What has been happenning to inequality? If all three of these have declined from high levels, then beyond doubt that has been a period of development for the country concerned. If one or two of these Central problems have been growing worse, ecspecially if all three have, it would be strange to call the result 'development' even if per capita income doubled".[6] Recently, the concept of economic development has been further widened. In this process world Development Report, 1991 states, "the Challenge of developemnt is to improve the quality of life. Especially in the world's poor countries, a better quality of life generally calls for higher incomes but it involves much more. It encompasses as ends in themselves better education, higher standards of health and nutrition, less poverty, a cheaner environment more equality of opportunity." Prof. Amartya Sen is also of the same view. He asserts, "the Purpose of development is to create an environment in which all people can expand their capabilities and opportunities can be enlarged for both present and future generations."[7] Thus, economic development is considered to be a wider concept than the economic growth. Here also the Development Economics of the West has been engulfed with a strange contradiction. Agreeing upon the difference between growth and development concepts in technical terms, practically, at the stage of the formulation of growth models and economic policies, most of the economists have defined growth and development synonymously. Despite acknowledging development to be ahead of the increase in income and production they define it only in terms of increase in income and production. The gist of all the definitions given by different economists is that development is a process whereby there is a continuous increase in productive capacity and per capita real GDP of a country in the long run and it reaches a higher level of living as compared to that of the earlier period. In this way they wished for differentiating development from growth, but they failed in it. They are being unable in giving a wider base and broader dimension to development even though they wish for it. Despite not acknowledging development in terms of mere increase in per capita GDP, they distinguish the developed, underdeveloped and developing countries only on the basis of per capita GDP. What kind of irony is this-on one side they view that it is not the development, but on another side they acknowledge that is development which in actuality is not? It seems that in regard to the concept of development there is a wide illusion, confusion and contradiction in the whole Western Economics.

Measures or indices of development

In Development Economics doubts and controversies with regard to measurement and indices of development is much more than that of its meaning and definition. It won't be wrong if we say that the controversy about the meaning and definition of development has basically emerged from the controversy regarding measurement and indices of development itself. The question is: can the development be measured quantitatively? Western economics has accepted that the quantitative measurement of development is possible. Having accepted this premise, the second question arises: how and by which parameters can the development be measured? That is, what are those indices or indicators, on the basis of which it can be stated that a country has developed and how much development could take place? From time to time a number of indices have been suggested for the measurement of development. It will be useful to know about these different indices of development and their limitations too. We can classify these different indices of development into two broad groups: - economic indicators and non-economic indicators.

(A) Economic indicators

1. Gross Domestic Product (GDP):

Some of the economists such as Kuznets, Mayer and Baldwin, Meed etc presume that real GDP is the best possible indicator of development. According to them, we can measure the rate of development on the basis of the rate of increase in real GDP. Despite being the useful measure of development to some extent, GDP can not be accepted as the most appropriate measure of development. Its main drawbacks are as follows:

(i) If in a country, the rate of growth of population is higher than the rate of growth of GDP then the per capita GDP and availability of goods and services will come down compared to the pervious period. It will then be ironic to proclaim in such a situation that the country has developed.

(ii) It is possible that the growth of GDP may be due to the increase in income of rich people only. Thus we are unable to get any information regarding income distribution with the help of GDP only.

(iii) If the growth of GDP has occurred due to the increase in the production of war-goods then also it cannot be regarded as development.

2. Per capita GDP:

Most of the economists believe that the growth of per capita GDP is the best, practicable and suitable measure of development. Kindelberger, Mayer, Higgins, Harvey Lebenstien, W.A. Lewis, Jacob Winer etc are all of the same opinion. Even the United Nations Organization has also accepted this measure. After accepting per capita GDP as the measure of development the impact of population increase is automatically taken into consideration because per capita GDP is calculated as total GDP divided by the total population. But as the measure of development, per capita GDP too is an incomplete unit of measurement and has many drawbacks as well. Among them, some of the main drawbacks are as follows:

(i) When we accept per capita GDP as the measure of development, many times we are entrapped into a strange situation. If both population and GDP of country have risen at the same rate, then too we will have to state that the country has not developed. In the same way, if the population of a country declines because of some reasons and GDP remains constant then it would have to be stated that the country has developed.

(ii) Because per capita GDP is an average measure, even after increase in per capita GDP it is possible that the rich may become richer and the poor would become poorer. If the growth of per capita GDP has occurred due to increase in the incomes of the rich people only then also there will be no improvement in the consumption and the standard of living of the common man of the country. Therefore, confusion may arise by accepting the growth of per capita GDP as the measure of economic development.

(iii) It is not necessary that the growth of per capita GDP too results in the increase in the quantity of per capita consumption. It is possible that the people may start to save more than before or the government may spend more for the military purposes from the increased income.

(iv) As a result of increase in per capita real GDP too, it is possible that the number of people living below the poverty line in the country may rise.

Limitations of GDP and per capita GDP both as measure of development

We have explained above some of the defects and deficiencies of accepting GDP and per capita GDP as measures of development. Besides, there are some other limitations also for which the GDP and per capita GDP can not be accepted as the measure of development.

(i) There is no universally accepted definition of GDP. So far, no satisfactory solution has been found out to the question of what should be included and what should not be included in the estimation of GDP.

(ii) In many countries at the time of estimation of GDP, a number of commodities of non- monetized sector are not taken into account. Self consumption and commodities and services that are not brought to the market for exchange are not properly calculated in the national income. For example, till today a large part of the exchange takes place without the use of money in the villages of some countries like India. The farmers receive clothes, utensils, articles made of wood and other services in exchange of grains. Similarly the farmers keep a large share of their produce for their self consumption. All these commodities are not brought to the market for sale and hence, these commodities are often omitted in the estimation of national income. Similarly unpaid services are also not taken into account in the calculation of national income. For example, when a house-maid cooks food or washes clothes for payment, all these services become part of the national income. But the same services performed by a housewife are not included in the national income. In spite of producing similar services in one situation they are included in national income whereas in another situation they are excluded. No satisfactory solution to this difficulty has, hitherto, been found out. In the same way, there has still been controversy on the issue of including administrative and defense services in the national income.

(iii) The calculation of GDP of different countries is done in the currencies of respective countries. Therefore, it is required to express them in terms of a single currency at the time of comparison to the GDPs of different countries and it is done with the help of the foreign exchange rate. But no foreign exchange rate can perform this function in an appropriate manner.

(iv) Difficulty also arises because of changes in the prices at the time of calculation of real GDP.

(v) The data related to GDP in underdeveloped countries are insufficient, incomplete and unreliable. Hence, proper measurement of development is not possible on the basis of such data.

(vi) This is also possible that for the increase in income, the health of the people would have been badly affected and moral, social and other problems would have also cropped up.

It is because of all these limitations that most of the economists do not acknowledge any of these two (i.e. GDP and per capita GDP) as an accurate measure of development.

Recently in an article Sanjeev Sanyal has also emphatically said that "GDP as a measure of human progress is outdated."[8]

3. Per capita Consumption

Some of the experts opine that the ultimate aim of development is to increase the standard of living of the people and the standard of living depends on the quantity of commodities and services available for consumption. Hence, the level of per capita consumption is the best measure of economic development. But this measure has also the difficulties of its own. The necessity of capital formation and savings is realized in every country in order to produce more in future and consumption is to be curtailed for this purpose. If a country has been increasing savings and capital formation by reducing its consumption then by acknowledging the per capita consumption as the measure of development, we cannot say that the country is moving on the path of economic development. On the other hand, if a country increases its present level of consumption but its savings and capital formation decline, then the possibility of declining in its total production will emerge in the future. But if we assume the per capita consumption level as the measure of development, then we have to say that the economic development of the said country has taken place.

4. Economic Welfare

According to some experts, economic welfare alone can be the best measure of economic development. While discussing economic development, we will not merely see what and how much is being produced. Rather we will also see that how is it being produced and distributed. In economic welfare the relative importance of the commodities which are being produced in the country has also to be kept in mind. In this way we have to take the value judgment. Likewise the social cost of production has also to be viewed. Although the measure of economic welfare is the more appropriate measure of development yet still the economists have not put it in practice. For this, they have given the reason that the value judgment, just distribution, social cost etc. are such terms that are practically very difficult to calculate. Therefore, the measure of economic welfare has been abandoned considering it to be impractical.

5. Adjusted GNP Measure

In view of the convenience for the comparative study among different countries, some economists have suggested to accept the Adjusted G.N.P. as a measure of development. The concept of purchasing power parity is applied to adjust the accounts of national income through this measure. In order to give an appropriate measure of economic welfare, Nordhos and Tobin have done the adjustment of G.N.P. For this purpose, the value of consumer durable commodities, excluding the expenses incurred in leisure and waste from the GNP, is added in the GNP after deducting an approximate amount meant for the defense expenditure and for the inconvenience of urbanization. They have reclassified expenditure on education and health as expenditure on investment rather than on consumption. But all the limitations of the measurement of national income are inherent in this measure also. Moreover, it is not a simple task to do the adjustment in the national income; it has its own difficulties and limitations.

6. Other Measures

Besides the above mentioned measures of development, some economists have suggested the use of other measures also. For example, reduction in the percentage of the poor section in the total population can be a good measure of economic development. According to these economists, the benefit of the development process should go to the poor section. Dr. V.K.R.V. Rao was of the opinion that if the poor people do not get any benefit during the process of development then it can not be accepted as economic development at all.

Some scholars like Colin Clark regard the changes that have taken place in the occupational structure of an economy as the measure of economic development. According to them, we can say that a country is undergoing economic progress if in any country the share of the primary sector is declining and the share of the secondary and tertiary sectors go on increasing in its occupational structure. Some economists view the rate of capital formation as an important measure of economic development. According to them, capital helps in increasing productivity; therefore, it can be an important measure of development. In this order, the per-man-hour productivity can also be an index of development. In the same way, some environmentalists have suggested a new measure called GDBR (Growth Destruction of Basic Resources) in order to measure the development.

All these measures are one-sided and an inherent assumption is working behind all these measures that development can be measured mathematically on the basis of economic considerations. Its wider dimensions and the delicate matters of the emotional world have so far been neglected.

Non-economic (social) indicators

Social indices have been presented in terms of the basic necessities of man. The main social indices include- life expectancy, calorie-intake, infant-mortality rate, enrolment in primary schools, shelter, nutrition, health and other such things which are related to the basic needs of a man. Their combined name is- The Basic Needs Approach about Economic Development. For the first time this approach was given by the World Bank's first mission constituted for the underdeveloped countries and this gained popularity since 1970. In 1976 the International Labour Organisation provided more popularity to this approach. The main purpose of this approach is to increase in productivity of labour and eliminate poverty of the people. A number of indices have been evolved to measure the development in accordance with this approach and the prominent ones are given as follows:

1. Social Accounting System: This system was propounded by Stone and Sayers. Piatt and Rhode had also propounded an index called social accounting matrix. But the unavailability of reliable and useful data is the main deficiency of this kind of system. Moreover, it is also difficult to include in it all the aspects of social development.

2. Composite Social Development Index: This index was developed by the United Nations

Research Institute on Social Development (UNRISD). Initially 73 indices were examined and finally 16 indices were selected from them. These indices are:

(i) Life expectancy at birth

(ii) The percentage of growth of population in the areas with a population of 20,000 or more

(iii) Per capita, per day consumption of animal protein

(iv) The total number of students enrolled at primary and secondary level

(v) Occupational enrolment ratio

(vi) Average number of individuals per room

(vii) News paper per 1000 population

(viii) The percentage of economically active population having electricity, gas, water etc

(ix) Per man agriculture-labour agricultural production

(x) Percentage of adult male-labour in agriculture

(xi) Per capita kilowatt consumption of electricity

(xii) Per capita consumption of steel (in kg.)

(xiii) Per capita consumption of energy

(xiv) Gross domestic product obtained from manufacturing work (in percentage)

(xv) Per capita foreign trade

(xvi) Percentage of wage and salary earners in economically active total population.

It becomes clear by looking at the above indices that these indices also can not be the appropriate measure of development. These indices have many deficiencies. Through them an attempt has been made to measure development in terms of structural changes instead of human welfare; more importance has been given to the measurement of inputs instead of production and many indices are such that they have no relevance in the context of the poor countries. In reality, an implicit assumption is working behind it that the poor countries of today should also develop only in the direction to today's developed counties, which is impossible, impractical and incongruous.

In the sequence of the indices of development, Drewnowski and Scott had suggested a new measure called Level of Living index in 1966. The Level of Living Index was defined in terms of the level of satisfaction of wants of the people. This can be measured by the flow of goods and services consumed by the people per unit of time. In it, the basic necessities of man have been divided into two categories-physical needs like nutrition, shelter and health and cultural needs like education, leisure and security etc.

3. Physical Quality of Life Index (PQLI) :

Moris D. Moris had given this index of development in 1979. Three indices were included in it (i) Life expectancy at the age of one year (ii) infant mortality and (iii) literacy.

This index is also incomplete. It is because many social and psychological indices have not been included in it, like security, justice, human rights etc.

4. Kuznets's analysis on the features of modern economic growth :

Kuznets explicated seven prominent features of modern economic growth-

(i) Rapid increase in per capita production

(ii) High growth rate of productivity

(iii) High rate of structural changes

(iv) Urbanization and industrialization

(v) Speedy social and ideological changes

(vi) The modern nations' approach of looking at outside countries and

(vii) International flow of physical and human capital.

Thus, as far as indicators for measurement of development are concerned, again we find diverse opinions. Different measures have been suggested by different economists, but in actual practice it is the per capita income, which is taken as the index for the measurement of both economic growth and economic development. It is on this basis that the economies of the world have been classified into developed economies, developing economies and undeveloped economies and all the countries of the world have been ranked accordingly. Thus the distinction between economic growth and economic development withers away for all practical purposes. Though everybody accepts that per capita income cannot be a true index of development, yet it is being used for constructing all sorts of growth models.

A New measure of Development: Human Development Index

This discussion of various measures and indices of development took a new turn when the first Human Development Report was published in 1990. In this report human development index, as a new measure, was proposed to measure the development. Explaining the importance of human development index, the human development report of 1995 says

"The concept of human development reinforces the belief that people should participate in the development process and benefit from it. Going beyond stabilization and economic growth, this broader vision of development has significantly influenced the development policy debates and dialogues. National soul-searching has moved human development concerns to the centre of national policy debates in many countries. What is the meaning of growth if it is not translated into the lives of people? In the era of opening markets and globalization of trade, does the comparative advantage of developing countries not rest on an intelligent investment in their people? Can development be sustainable if people do not take part in the processes that influence their lives? Are there no alternatives to conventional wisdom in setting development priorities, managing the process and distributing the outcome?"[9]

Human development concept focuses on the entire society, not just the economy. It is erected on four essential pillars- productivity, equity, sustainability and empowerment. It states that the purpose of development is to create an enabling environment for people to enjoy long, healthy and creative life. Thus, this human development concept is a new development paradigm and an alternative to GNP growth theories. It is much broader than the conventional theories of economic development.

The Human Development Index (HDI) was constructed to reflect the important dimensions of human development. The HDI contains three indicators: life expectancy representing a long and healthy life; educational attainment representing knowledge; and real GDP, representing a decent standard of living. The HDI is thus an alternative to GDP per capita, and it is increasingly being used to monitor the progress of nations and of global society. Now the countries of the world are ranked on the basis of HDI value. However, with the use of HDI, an interesting phenomenon and contradiction has also emerged in the field of measurement of development. Till now per capita real GDP has been used practically as the measurement of development and on the basis of it, the development order of various countries of the world has been constantly determined too. The HDI ranking of countries differs significantly from the ranking by real GDP per capita. This paradox is illustrated in the table below:[10]

RANKING OF THE COUNTRIES

	COUNTRY	*HDI RANK*	*REAL GDP PER CAPITA RANK*
1.	CANADA	1	8
2.	USA	2	1
3.	JAPAN	3	8
4.	NETHERLANDS	4	20
5.	FINLAND	5	24
6.	SPAIN	9	29
7.	SWITZERLAND	13	2
8.	GERMANY	15	6
9.	HONG KONG	24	10
10.	COSTA RICA	28	60
11.	URUGUAY	32	53
12.	SINGAPORE	35	16
13.	U.A.E.	45	4
14.	FIJI	46	63
15.	INDIA		

Now the question is: out of these two measures, i.e. GDP and HDI, which is more appropriate? No definite answer is available in the Western Economics. Further, the inadequacy of the concept of HDI has been accepted by the Human Development Report itself. It states:

"It (HDI) is not a measure of well being. Nor is it a measure of happiness..... To give a more complete picture of human development in any country, the HDI must be supplemented with other important human development indicators."[11]

"The HDI- though much broader than GNP should still be regarded as partial measure of human progress. It should thus be supplemented by other qualitative and quantitative studies of aspects of human progress for example, political freedom, cultural progress or improved physical environment."[12]

Thus it seems that there is utter confusion and wide controversy among the modem economists with regard to the concept and measurement of development. In reality all the measures presented by Western Economics are proving themselves to be incomplete, one-sided, confusing and sometimes suicidal and destructive. The whole western concept of development is not consistent with human happiness and well-being. Development cannot and should not simply be defined in terms of GNP, total or per Capita, or in terms of per capita availability of goods and services, or in terms of HDI. It calls for a new approach, which can ensure the all round development of an integral man. If we regard development as a multi-dimensional, integrated and all-inclusive concept then many indicators will have to be taken to the development and changes will have to be made in the list and priorities of these indicators in accordance to time and place.

5. Questions and inconsistencies arising out of western development philosophy and model

The Western development philosophy and model has given rise to so many questions and hence a very big question mark has been suffixed to the whole

Western thought. These questions seem to have no answers, or whatever answers exist are bound to negate this philosophy and model itself. These questions are becoming so deep and serious that leaving them aside, there can not be any thinking about development. To understand the direction of these questions here, we are giving some prominent questions below:

(a) What is the exact meaning of development and are the current theories of development able to explain the development process?

(b) Will it be appropriate to accept the meaning of development as 'industrialization' and 'urbanization'?

(c) Can development be understood and measured in terms of the increase in the per capita real GDP?

(d) Can everything be purchased by money? Can wealth be accepted as the highest purpose of man's life? Can all the problems of life be resolved by accumulating more and more wealth? Is there always a positive correlation between wealth (or more production of goods) and happiness?

(e) Can we find solution to all our present-day problems by the conceptual framework and behavioural assumptions presented by the Western development philosophy?

(f) Can there be the same development model for all countries and for all times?

(g) Should we also follow the path of industrialization by dismantling the co-ordinance of nature for our development as the West does?

(h) Why and how is the present development process allowed to continue excessive affluences together with extreme poverty among the various countries, among the different regions of the same country and among different parts of the same city?

(i) Are the various activities of the rich countries helping in fulfilling the aspirations of the development of the poor nations or impeding the process? If helpful, how and to which extent?

(j) What are the sources of national and international prosperity and who has been benefited from such prosperity and why?

(k) How did the poor countries of the world get trapped into debt and who did so? Is there any relation between this debt trap and the present direction of development? What are the implications of this debt trap from the point of view of the economies of the rich countries?

(l) How do foreign debt, foreign aid and foreign capital-investment affect the economies of the poor and rich countries and what are their implications?

(m) To which extent, in which areas and on what terms should the foreign multinational companies be given the freedom to work in the poor countries?

(n) Is the international trade system in the name of globalization desirable for the sake of development of the poor countries? Who is getting the maximum benefit from such trade?

(o) Can more production, more consumption and more trade be called a right step in the direction of development?

(p) Is it desirable, beneficial, and practical to adopt the present life style of the West from the point of view of development?

Two Big Questions

By adopting this Western development model whatever has been achieved in the name of development by a few countries of the world gives rise to two questions :-

1. Is it really the development which makes man happy?

2. Is it possible and practicable to make available this type of development to all the persons of all the countries of the world or in other words, is it a practicable and sustainable development path?

When we enquire into these questions in the light of facts, we find the answer to both the questions to be negative. In their lust for development, the countries taking to the Western model have not only created dangerous situations for their own existence but also endangered the entire mankind. The environment around us is getting more and more polluted due to air, water and soil pollution. Not only this, even human relations, sentiments and sensitivities are also being debased. In the last hundred years and especially in the last four decades the whole of the earth has come on the verge of catastrophe. The temperature of the earth is continuously increasing owning to the green house effect. The temperature of the earth increases due to the green house gases exasperated by burning coal, natural gas and oil. Because of the increase in the temperature of the earth, the sea level may increase and may become shallow for the states which have settled near the seas. The ozone layer which acts as a safeguard of the earth by preventing disastrous and sharp ultra-violet rays coming from the sun continues being slender. There has occurred a big hole in the layer above the Antarctica Island. Besides, we have also come to know that hole appears on the upper atmosphere of Australia and New Zealand in some months of the year. According to an estimate, from 1970 the quantity of ozone is depleting by the rate of 1.5% per annum. The conclusion of the scientific studies is that the main reason behind the depletion of ozone is the mischievous activities of modern man involved in the blind-run for materialistic comfort and convenience. One of the prominent reasons for the decay of the ozone layer is the production of chemicals in the group of chlorofluoro carbon which is being increasingly used in the industries like refrigerators, air conditioning, tools, plastics, foams, colour, aero-sol etc. The second important reason for the depletion of the ozone layer is the unrestrained cutting of plants and trees for urbanization and industrialization. Now the Western intellectuals have also started accepting the destructive effects of present technology and model of development. Today, whatever problems we witness in the form of fast destruction of natural resources, energy crisis, destruction of forests, reduction in the level of ground water, irregularities in the climate and rainfall, soil erosion, decline in man's moral and human values, lack of peace and happiness, increasing violent tendency and all such other problems are basically inherent in the Western model of development. Therefore, by no parameter, it can be called the development that gives peace and happiness to the human being.

Here it would be pertinent to ponder over the cost at which the affluent countries have been able to reach their present standard of living. That is to say, how much burden is being borne by the world on account of their level of living? The rich countries having 20% of the world population consume 80% of the total world resources to maintain their production–structure, consumption pattern and life style. They posses 50% of the total geographical area, consume 60% of the energy and monopolise 85% of the income of the whole world. An average American consumes more than 2 tonnes of steel in the form of cars, 112 kgs of meat and around 8000 kgs of oil every five years. According to another estimate, each American consumes per day articles equivalent to the weight of his body. An American child under 13 years of age spends annually 230 dollars as pocket money which is more than the average per capita income of most of the developing countries of the world. To maintain their level of production and consumption, these rich countries of the world throw in the atmosphere 80% CFCs in the form of green house gases. In this, the share of the U.S.A. alone is more than 22%. Again, America produces a huge amount of aluminum waste annually which is sufficient enough to produce 6000 jet planes. The oil consumption per unit of output in America is 16 times to that of India.

All these facts make it amply clear that if all the countries of the world take the standard of living of the developed countries of the West, particularly America, as the object of their development, it would be well-nigh impossible to achieve this aim with the help of the world resources known up till now. Besides, the environment will be irreparably poisoned as a result of mass production of green house gases if this development technology is adopted by all the countries of the world. Contemplation of life under these circumstances portends a gruesome scenario. Hence, the present technology is neither practicable nor sustainable.

On both theoretical and practical grounds, now many inconsistencies, deficiencies and weaknesses of the development model of the West have come to the limelight. The astonishing fact is that in spite of being surrounded by these ever emerging crises because of this model of development, neither the West is able to come out from it nor the inclination of the rest of the world to adopt this model has decreased. Yet at some places protests to negate it are coming to the limelight and the intellectuals of the Western world themselves seem to warn against the horrific dangers of this development path. Similarly, many countries of Asia and Africa have also started searching their own path in accordance to their nature. It will be useful to know about the inconsistencies, deficiencies and weaknesses of the Western model before considering the new path. A brief-summary of these inconsistencies has been presented below:-

1. The present development model is exploitative. It has given rise to the process of exploitation of one unit by the other at all the levels. For example, the sequence of the exploitation as village by town, town by city, poor state by prosperous state, poor and the primary goods producing countries by prosperous industrial countries, most of the world by the multi national companies, consumers by producers, one small producer (or company) by big producer (or company) is the outcome of this model. In reality, the tendency of making their own development by exploiting others is the inherent feature of this model. Whatever development today's Western Europe and America have gained is due to the exploitation of the colonies by their imperial regimes.

If England had not acquired the resources from India in the form of economic drainage her Industrial Revolution would not have succeeded. Thus this model is based upon the assumption of assuming the exploitation necessary for development. Therefore, it cannot become the medium for exploitation-less development.

2. The Market regulated economy of the Western development model is based on the approach of moving forward, by taking advantage of others' helplessness, by charging higher price or by giving less wages or imposing their terms in the trade (exchange). The healthy mechanism of development for all cannot proliferate from it.

3. Unlimited desires and wants, tendency for more and more production, wide spread trade, the search for market for selling goods, struggle, war and imperialism (political or economic) to occupy market, raw materials and sources of energy, and all such things originate from this Western development process. The history of the world of the last three hundred years is the testimony to this tendency.

4. The assumption of economic rationality has led to the tendency of maximally utilizing the resources as soon as possible by applying the technology to its maximum possible level. In reality, it is regarded as the only path of achieving high rate of development. That is why the hard sciences and the approaches that have emerged from them are being given priority in place of soft sciences. As a result, moral and social concerns keep on receding.

It is because of the lack of human and moral direction to economic prosperity and new technology that the social and psychological dangers are percolating in the prosperous countries and societies of today.

The process of disintegration of the family has been sped up by the increasing infringe in marital relations in the developed nations. According to Human Development report of 1994, during 1987-91 the marriages which ended in divorces are 43% in Canda, 58% in Finland, 49% in Denmark, 48% in Sweden and America, 45% in Norway and 42% in Britain. During 1985-92, the children born due to extra-marital relations were 52% in America and 47% in Denmark. In the sphere of crime and criminality, America has become the number one country in the whole world. In America, there are 8 murders, 118 rape cases, 234 crimes relating to toxic drugs and 426 people being imprisoned per one lakh population in a year. In 1993, the number of crimes reported to the police was one crore forty lakhs. According to the Business Week magazine, due to such crimes there is loss of 4, 35,000 crore dollars. In America, every year, more than 20 lakhs of girls become pregnant before their marriage. Among them, the number of girls becoming pregnant in adolescence is 10 lakh in a year. The seriousness of the situation can be understood by the point that Lead Will, an institution of Coloredy, rewards unmarried girls who keep themselves free from pregnancy, with a dollar per day. In the area of New Heaven it was decided to distribute condoms among children in the schools. In the same way, in America, 75% of the total deaths of men are due to murder, suicide and driving cars in a drunken state.

Moreover there are the cases of one murder in every 21 minutes and rape of one woman in every 16 seconds. 80 lakh adolescent boys and girls do necessarily drink wine once in a week, 2 crore people are engrossed with nerve related diseases, 10 lakh students drop out every year from schools and colleges because of emotional problems, more than 3 lakh people attempt to commit suicide every year and among them 56 thousand become successful. In the same way 1,400 people in a population of one lakh become victims of road accidents in a year. The suicide cases per one lakh population are 58 in Hungary, 49 in Finland, 35 in Australia and 34 in Switzerland, as registered during 1989-1991. According to another report, the data of United Nations Organization shows that 34% marriages in 31 industrial nations ends in divorces and the birth of 17% children takes place due to extra-marital relations. At per one lakh population, 48 rapes, 5 murders and 21 suicides occur in a year. Some people predicted to such an extent that the collapse of American society will take place due to spreading culture of Tygon, cellular phones and drugism.

5. The use of mathematical formulae in the development model has made the whole of the development process and development policy impractical and due to this, dehumanization of economics and economic thought has started. According to Prof. Amartya Sen, the engineering aspect (allocation–skill) of economics began to be given priority over its moral aspect (social responsibility). As a result, the whole of the development-path has gone astray.

6. The Western economic thought acknowledged development, in terms of more production and high per capita income, to be its aim-in a way means itself has been regarded as aim. As the means and ends are not being differentiated properly exploitation, atrocity and maltreatment are getting a prime place in the society in various forms and shapes. This is the ambiguity of this development thought.

7. Present development-economics is market centered. In it, more goods are produced for the rich people endowed with more purchasing power. Many extravagant and misleading methods such as advertisement, marketing etc have come up to motivate these rich people to purchase more and more commodities. It has created duality and contradictions in the economy. On the one hand there are rich people who are not only motivated, encouraged and excited but also misled and bamboozled to purchase more commodities of different kinds even without their requirements. More interesting is that the increase in demand of this kind is presumed as the motivating force of development. On the other hand, there are poor persons who have pressing demands but they are forced not to be able to purchase and thus they are deprived of even the commodities of their basic requirement.

8. The present method of development and technology is reverse (or invert) and is going to

beget crisis for itself. In this system the means which are deficient are attempted to utilize to the maximum with the intention of enhancing the level of production. Consequently, the economic system is put to the state of resource-crisis. For instance, there is deficiency of energy. Yet it adopts the production-technique that uses more energy; hence it results into energy-crisis. There is inadequacy of water yet effort is made to increase production in agriculture by utilizing those varieties of seeds that need more water-hence water crisis emerges. Similarly, employment crisis is created by employing machine-based production techniques even in those countries where labour is abundant. In the same way, in spite of knowing the fact that the fertility of the land does not increase from the chemical fertilizers, only its stimulation is increased, still more and more chemical fertilizers are used that not only destroys the original fertility of the land but creates the problem of pollution also. New crises emerge out of the modus operandi adopted to resolve a particular crisis. Thus, the whole development methodology is proving itself to be the creator and upholder of crisis.

9. The Human Development Report of 1996 has revealed the incompatibilities of the present development to be an eye opener. It has been clearly acknowledged in this report that no automatic relationship is found between the economic growth based on per capita GDP and

the human development, which means that the increase in the rate of economic growth does not necessarily lead us in the direction of human development. The present philosophy, approach and direction of development have given birth to that kind of development as a result of which the problem has been made much more complicated rather than resolving it. The report mentions five varieties of such development as Jobless development, Merciless development, Voiceless development, Rootless development and Futureless development.[13]

Jobless development means that there is a fast increase in the Gross Domestic Product but in comparison to it, employment opportunities do not increase to a sufficient extent. For example, in the Sixth Plan (1980-85), the rate of annual increase of Gross Domestic Product in India was 5.7 per cent whereas the rate of increase in employment was 1.7 per cent only and in the Seventh Plan these were 5.8 per cent and 1.9 per cent respectively. During Eighth and Tenth Plan period also the rate of increase in employment was inconceivably low as compared to the Gross Domestic product.

What is more engaging, is that during the Plan Period, the rate of increase in employment is also noticed to be lagging behind the rate of increase in labour force. Notwithstanding all the development plans and increase in production, the number of unemployed persons has been continuously rising in the country, the main reason being that we did not concede employment as the central goal of development in our Plans; rather we considered it merely as the bi-product of development.

Merciless Development refers to the development where the benefits of development largely go to the affluent sections and no improvement occurs in the number and condition of the poor in the country. For example, 39.3 per cent (31.3 crores) of the population was registered below the poverty line in 1987-88. Later on even after many years in 1993-94 also, 37 per cent (32.crores) of the population was below the poverty line. Even at present nearly 26 crore people are living below the poverty-line in India. Similarly, the number of inhabitants in the J.J. Colonies and slums in the urban areas has been on the increase. What kind of development is this as a consequence of which the assets and the luxurious goods, already with the rich sections, have been increasing and whereas on the other side, a vast section of the population is forced to live a life on miseries and poverty? This surely reflects the cruelty of the development process.

Voiceless Development is the development where the evolution of democracy does not cope up with the pace of economic development. In it, the right of ownership of property is not available to the poorer section of the population as well as adequate opportunities for education, health and skill development also remain largely unavailable to them. For example, a denial of land-ownership rights to the landless farmers, a wide difference between the female and male literacy rate, difference in the availability of educational facilities and educational attainment of the rich and the poor sections of the population, malnutrition, non-availability of other essential facilities of life to the scheduled castes, scheduled tribes and other backward section of the population- all these symptoms are enough to indicate the state of voiceless development.

Rootless Development represents that development which alienates the population from their own cultural identity and roots. Indiscriminate construction of dams, canals, large factories, railway lines etc by assuming them as the only symbols of development. As a result of this sometimes a large chunk of population become refugees and are deprived from their homes and livelihood. This kind of situation emerges because of imitating the development plans parallel with that of the Western countries without giving a serious thought to the development of traditional alternative means.

Futureless Development is the development that indicates towards the system in which the present generation misappropriates the resources required for the future generation. For instance, irrational use of different minerals, such as iron, zinc, copper, led, aluminums etc and energy resources, increasing in the area of barren land as a consequence of not protecting its fertility, unrestrained deforestation etc will ultimately finish the possibility of future development.

Besides, we can designate this development as a *Sanskarhin Vikas* (uncultured development) because of the total decline of the moral and human values and disintegration of family and community life.

There is an urgent need to stop this development and take it in the right direction. That is why the Human Development Report (1996) has recommended that India should adopt such a development process which can pave the way for employment-generating development, egalitarian development, cooperative development, grassroots development and nourishing development. Over and above this we would have to also pay more attention towards the *Sanskarit Vikas* (cultured development) in the coming days.

What is required for the proper evaluation of the currently prevalent development model is that we should enquire that where the world has reached and what has it received from the development path adopted by it.

In this regard, the Human Development Reports of 1995 and 1996 have made available very important informations.

There is no second opinion that now the world has become richer than it was before and it has got spectacular achievements also in many fields. The total income of the world had increased from 4 trillion to 23 trillion dollar during 1950-92 and the per capita income has increased even more than three fold. Extraordinary works have been accomplished in the field of technology especially in the fields of information, telecommunication and medicine. Moreover, there is an improvement in the facilities of education, health and transportation. The mortality rate has declined and the average life expectancy has witnessed an increase. Production in both agriculture and industry has expanded and the articles for luxurious and conspicuous consumption have also puffed up. In spite of all these achievements the world has been engrossed and immersed in many problems and new problems are cropping up every day. Whatever we have thought of in regard to development has not happened and in its place something else has happened and whatever has happened really presents an extremely horrible picture. Even today, we live in such a world where a large chunk of the population is a victim of the problems of hunger, poverty, unemployment and inequality. We are living in the midst of strange contradictions-some countries are starving whereas others are wasting the food grains. The inequality between the rich and the poor countries is continuously increasing. 80 per cent population of the poor countries of the world has got the share of only 16 per cent in the total income of the world and on the other hand, the mere 20 per cent of the population of the rich countries has got hold over 84 per cent of the global income. The Human Development Report of 1996 has explicated that the condition of 89 countries has aggravated compared to the last 10 years as a result of which the inequalities have widened between the rich and the poor countries. The report also warns that the economic inequalities between the industrialized and developing countries will turn out to be inhuman, crossing beyond the limits of inequality if the same trend continues. The unemployment crisis has been on the rise. Even in the rich industrial countries nearly 35 million people are in search of employment and in poor countries employment will have to be generated amongst about 1 billion people in the next decade.[14]

The situation of the developing countries is much more worrisome. In these countries, around 17 million people die due to infectious diseases, 800 million people do not get sufficient food and 500 million people are victims of malnutrition. About 1.3 billion people (around one-third of the population) are living below the poverty line, 130 million children at the primary level and 275 million children at the secondary level can not go to the schools. Besides it, not only the infant mortality rate and maternal mortality rates are very high as also the birth rate. The whole scenario of these countries is very critical and painful. The empty and dry belly, nude or semi-nude body, faded eyes and squeezed cheeks, the wandering skeleton of the people inflicted by many diseases, look like a manifestation of poverty itself. Here we can easily view in great number, the children tormented of hunger, people crying from pain, mothers dying due to the pain of delivery and unemployed youths wandering with pain from door to door in search of jobs, dirty slums, fractured J.J. Colonies, clay made homes tapping in the rain and burning in the sun in which humans and animals both live together. Thus the poverty of these countries is not only the poverty it seems to be, but the refutation of the human existence itself.

On the other hand, the condition of the prosperous, industrial countries of the world is also not so well and is continuously deteriorating. In these countries more than 15 lakh people are the victims of AIDS. Total unemployment rate is 8 per cent while the unemployment rate among the youths is 15 per cent. The share of 40 per cent of the poorest families is only 18 per cent in the total income, 100 million people are below the poverty line and more than 5 million people do not have houses to live. More than one-third of the marriages end in divorces and each year, 1, 30, 000 rapes are eventualized. The destruction of the jungles in Europe due to air pollution is leading to the loss equivalent to 35 million dollars in a year. Thus, on the whole, it seems that the chariot of development has come to a halt somewhere or it has gone astray. Today's necessity is that we should enquire as to why it has come to a halt or has gone astray and try to present a new alternative development philosophy by removing its defects and disorder.

In this regard Capra s observation on present development models and economy are worth noting, When he says – " An economy based on unlimited material consumption, excessive competition and on the reduction of all quality to quantity is not viable in the long sum and is bound to collapse sooner or later. If we internalise the costs of environmental degradation, social distruption like terrorism and war, the economic progress that we attained becomes far from the real progress".[15]

References

1. See Meier, Gerald M. and Rauch, James E., Leading Issues in Economic Development, 2007, p. 73.

2. Meier and Rauch, op. cit., p. 75.

3. Kindleberger, C.P.; Economic Development, 1977.

4. See Meier and Boldwin; Economic Development: Theory, History and Policy, 1957, p. 2; Kuznets, S.; Towards a Theory of Economic Growth in R. Lakachman (ed.); National Policy for Economic Welfare at Home and Abroad, p. 16; Baran, Paul A.; The Political Economy of Growth, 1957, p. 20; Rostow, W.W.; The Process of Economic growth, 1952, p. 81; Lewis, W.A.; The Theory of Economic Growth, 1955, p. 9; Kindleberger and Herrick, Economic Development, p.1.

5. Ahuja, H.L.; Macroeconomics, Theory and Policy, 2007, pp. 708-10; Misra, S.K. and Puri, V.K.; Indian Economy, 2004, pp. 5-6.

6. Seers, Dudley, "The Meaning of Development presented at the Eleventh World Conference of the Society for International Development, N. Delhi, 1969.

7. Sen, Amartya; Development as Freedom, Oxford University Press, 2001, p. 175.

8. Sanyal, Sanjeev, Institute of Policy Studies, Singapore; Go Beyond Statistics, Times of India, 10.2.2009.

9. Human Development Report, 1995, pp. 117-18.

10. Op. cit.

11. Op. cit., p. 12.

12. Op. cit., p. 121.
13. Human Development Report, 1996.
14. Op. cit.
15. Capra, Fritjof; Uncommon Wisdom; p. 258.

2

Search for a New Development Path

It seems that despite their spectacular achievements the learned elite of the world are not satisfied with this Western model and want to replace it with some other better socio-economic structure. Today, all kinds of 'isms' are becoming helpless in solving the basic problems of mankind happily and peacefully. After a long sequence of experiences of various approaches and policies, a dire necessity is being invariably felt for a new approach in the whole world. Renowned environmentalist and the Chairman, inter-governmental panel on climate change, Shri R.K. Pachauri is also of the view that it is high time to take a fresh approach to development. He observes, "The current economic crisis provides us with a timely opportunity to review our basic pattern of economic growth and development. Despite the warning that Mahatma Gandhi repeated on several occasions before and at the time of independence we have largely pursued a form of development that emulates that of the Western industrialised world. That this model is largely unsuited to our conditions is now becoming increasingly apparent to us. It is now seen as flawed even to citizens of the developed world. It is this model that has created high levels of economic disparity between different sections of society, particularly in North America, and Contiributed over whelmingly to the problem of human-induced climate change."[1] Similarly, Dr. V.R. Pachmukhi has also clearly stated that "Today, the world economy and in particular, the developing world is at its crossroads in its development struggle.....There are many new challenges for the professional world for conducting analytical and policy oriented research. We have to evolve our own indigneous paradigm of development, best suited for our social, institutional, political and cultural framework."[2] Hence, it is now high time to go beyond the Western model and try to develop a new path. Though it is a subject which demands deeper study and research, yet here an attempt is made to suggest and submit some of the broad dimensions of *Bharatiya* Approach of Development.

Dharma-guided Human Centered Holistic Mangal development Approach

The Concept of Sumangalam or Mangal Development

It has so far been clear from our hitherto deliberation that there are thorough and serious differences of opinion among the modern economists regarding the meaning, measurement, approach, direction and strategy of development. Over and above, all are in the state of confusion. They all seem to negate, after sometime, their own statements. The Western concept of development has no relationship with man's happiness and well-being. This faulty definition of development has made the simple and sober gentleman a prey to an imaginary and false presumption of poverty and destitute by assuming the maximum availability of commodities as the goal of development. The people who have grains to eat, water and milk to drink, simple cloths to wear and simple house to live, but do not have luxurious articles such as soda water, cigarette, wine, sofa, Kaleene, large buildings, T.V. car, refrigerator etc. are being regarded as under-developed or backward. Therefore, we have to change this defective definition of development. It calls for a new approach, which can ensure the all-round development of an integral man. In view of this, an attempt is made here, to present an alternative concept.

CONCEPTUAL TERMS

In modern economics many terms are being used such as economic development, economic growth, progress, human development, quality of life etc. But among all of them no term is capable of expressing the entire thought in a proper perspective. This shows the imperfectness of the prevalent conceptual terms. This imperfectness of term also leads to directional confusion. Mostly we use two terms- growth or development- but both of them are falling short or proving helpless. In order to get rid of this deficiency of the term, I have taken the help from the vocabulary of Indian language. In this regard I want to suggest the use of the term *Sumangalam* or '*Mangal* Development' in place of the present terms of 'development' or 'growth'. The concept of *Sumangalam* or (*Mangal* Development), as I feel, is more appropriate, correct, compatible and an all-inclusive concept and through this we can express in a better way whatever we have in mind.

The concept of *Sumangalam* can be defined in the following words: *Sumangalam* means a continuous, long – term rise in the standard of life of all the people in the country and thus raising the level of gross social happiness primarily by utilising country's own resources.

Or

Sumangalam means a sustainable, nourishing, well-cultured, egalitarian, integral, balanced and all-round development, by awakening the country's will and ability to work, primarily with the help of indigenous efforts, capabilities, resource-endowments and skills in the light of its eternal values of life and in the context of its expectations, aspirations, needs, nature and socio-economic conditions with a view to raise the standard of life and gross social happiness.

The main features of this definition: The above-mentioned definition of *Sumangalam* enumerates the following main features of this concept.

(1) The concept of *Mangal* (well-being) is very much present in the whole thought process and behaviour pattern of India. *Mangal* (well-being) has been desired at every level. Every Indian desires *mangal* and he expects from elderly persons the blessings for his *mangal*. Not only this, he wants *mangal* even from the entire nature. That is why he prays in these words[3] :

Prakriti Panchabhutani grahalokah swarastatha
Dishh kalashch sarvesham sada kurvantu mangalam

In our *Puranas*, the goddess Lakshmi has been referred to as *Mangala* and *Sumangala*. It means that we do not want only wealth but we want *mangal* wealth (or wealth endowed with well-being). The concept of *mangal* in Indian thought has been given so much importance that God is also called in the name of *mangala*. Therefore, in morning contemplation, it is recited as[4]:

Om sachidanand rupaya namostu paramatmane
Jyotirmaya swarupaya viswamangalya moortaye.

This is why, in the Hindu tradition, before the commencement of each work, the *mangala* form of God is eulogized by reciting the following hymn:

Mangalam bhagwaan Vishnu mangalam garudadhwajah,
Mangalam pundarikakshoh mangalaayatano Harih.

In Jain religion too, before the commencement of any work the following prayer is recited:

Mangalam bhagwaan viro, mangalam gautamo gani,
Mangalam Kundkudadyo dharmostu mangalam.

Sant Tulasidasji stated in Ram Charitamaanasa that the birth of Sri Ram was to do the world's *mangal*- '*Ram Janamu Jaga mangala hetu*'[5]. Not only that in the very first shloka of Baalkaanda of Ramcharitmaanas we find the word 'Mangalaanaam'. Further the whole text of Ramcharitmaanas is full of the terms like 'mangal', 'sumangal', 'Amangalhaari', 'mangaldaayak' etc. which shows that the central idea of Ramcharitmaanas is also of 'mangal'.

(2) Integral–Holistic World-view:- We know that the whole Western developmental thought is based upon fragmented, mechanistic reductionistic world-view based on the Cartesian-Newtonion philosophy. In this world view matter is regarded as the basis of all existence and the material world is taken as a multitude of separate parts assembled into a huge machine. Almost all the disciplines of knowledge have accepted this mechanistic reductionistic worldview and they have developed their theories, models and concepts on the basis of it. But now modern scientific community is becoming aware of the limitations of this view. And they are realising that this world-view is in all respect incompatible, impractical, useless and destructive. Contrary to it, from the very beginning, Indian thinkers have acknowledged an integral-holistic world-view. Now, the recent discoveries of science have proved that the universe (cosmos) is an integrated, integral and holistic unit. Quantum physics now clearly states that in the universe, the parts seeming to be separated are not only deeply and intimately connected and knitted with each other, rather they are part and parcel of one another. Consequently, a new concept of unbroken wholeness has emerged which negates this traditional thought that it is possible to deliberate and analyze the universe by assuming that it is a sum total of different separate parts. The Indian wise men had already visualized this truth and that is why they stated that *'yatpinde tatbrahmaande'* (that which is in microcosm is also in the macrocosm.) They believed that there is only one conscious element present in the whole world– *sarvam khalwamidam brahamh*. On the basis of it, it has been said that the individual, society and universe are not different and independent units, but the same single element is manifested at different levels. Among them, there is an organic relationship.

Therefore, monotony and harmony must remain between them. It will be wrong to assume that the world can objectively be interpreted and analyzed by remaining outside of it and maintaining a distance from it. This is a participatory universe. We are neither separate from it nor it can be so. The truth is that the emotional world controls and regulates the world of objects. The change in emotions necessarily makes changes in the objects also. On the basis of it, Indian intellectuals have stated that if one purifies and sanctifies oneself, the world will be compelled to be so.

With regard to this integral world view Capra's observations are also worth noting:

"The new concepts in Physics have brought about a profound change in our worldview from the mechanistic conception of Descartes and Newton to a holistic and ecological view, a view which I have found to be a similar to the views of mystics of all ages and traditions ..... To achieve this state of dynamic balance a radically different social and economic structure will be needed, a cultural revolution, in the true sense of the word. The survival of our whole civilization may depend on whether we can bring about such a change."[6] Thus Capra emphasises the " System theory" which looks at the world in terms of the interrelatedness and interdependence of all phenomena.

(3) Mangal Approach towards Nature-The Divine Mother or Deity

Today there is diserible concern all over the world about the growing pollution and deteriorating environment. The root cause of this problem is the fragmented mechanistic world-view. It is the belief that nature can be borken up in parts and dealt with in that fashion without causing any grave injury to it because it is like dismantling a machine at the most. Just we take out a part of a machine with the help of screwdriver and fit in another part, similarly, we can also deal with the different componens of nature. Needless to say such a belief has given rise to insensitivity towards nature. The english scientist Fracis Bacon Opined that nature is inanimate and it can be exploited no end. Man has the right to use it for his own good. This thinking was responsible for the development strategies involving triumphing and exploiting nature, which in turn, led to loss of environment.

Contrary to it, Bharatiya philosophy believes in holistic integral worldview according to which a mutually dependent, indivisible relationship exists in entire creation, nature and environment. The most important thing is our approach towards nature. In our tradition every Bharatiya looks upon nature as his/her mother or a deity. This approach stresses co-existence, harmony and cordiality with nature. If we succeed in re-establishing this approach, the whole system along with all postulates and our conduct would change. The materialistic thinkers of the west have failed to comprehend this viewpoint and have instead made fun of it. When the Bharatiya worships the earth, the cow, the Tulsi plant, the ganga and the trees, he is derided as one belonging to a primitive society. But now even the Westerners are beginning to understand the importance of nature. We do not treat nature as our rival and have no conflict with it. Consequently, there is no question of feeling proud in having secured victory over nature and treating it as maid. How can one compete with one's mother? Therefore, we think not in terms of exploiting but milking nature.

How should we look at nature and it should look at us this is the subject of a beautiful hymn in yajur veda. The rishi speaks, "Mitrasya Chakshusha Sarvaani bhutani sameekshantaam. Mitrasyaham Chakshusha sarvaani sameekshe. Mitrasya Chakshusha Sameekshamahe.[7] There are three important points covered in it. First, all living beings should look kindly at me. In otherwords this is a prayer to all elements in nature to do good to us, to be kind to us and to be friendly towards us. Secondly, the worshipper prays that he should look at nature in a friendly manner. This is the foundation of love of nature, techniques, technologies and conduct. Nature is our friend and not an enemy. The third point covered in the aforsaid prayer is that both of us, i.e., nature and man should look at each other in a friendly way. Thus, a divine mind, a divine viewpoint and motherly perception of nature and environment is deeply embedded in our culture. This very idea has been expressed in simple words in the *Raamcharitmanas "Jad chetan Jag Jeeva Sakal Ram-maya jaani Bandaun sakal pad kamal sada jori jug paani"* (Considering all that is inanimate or animate besides this world, all creatures and water as existing in Lord Rama (Rama-maya), may I ever bow to them!). This has been our sentiment towards nature and it has been reflected in different ways in our behaviour pattern. On the basis of this approach we have to construct a holistic mangal development path and a socio-economic-technological structure that can pull along harmoniously with nature rather than degenerate it. We shall have to make everyone aware of the importance of the following prayer that gives the message of harmony with the universe and nature: 'Om dyau shantih antriksham shantih, prithvi shantirapah shantih shantiroshadhayah shantih. Vanaspatyah shantirvishvedevah shantibramha shantih, Serva shantih, shantireva shantih, sa ma shantiredehi. Om shantih shantih shantih.[8] (May there be peace on the earth in the space and in the abode of gods. Let all elements governed by different gods be in peace. May all our herbs and Vegetation promote peace. Let there be peace everywhere and always. May this peace continue to swell!).

It is because of this change in approach towards nature that experts are emphasising on the integration of environment with development. For instance world Bank clearly states that

"The old notion of 'development versus environment' has given way to a new view in which better environmental stewardship is essential to sustain development."[9]

Similarly, Todaro and smith say that : "In recent years economists have become increasingly aware of the important implications of environmental issues for the success of development efforts.....Rising pressures on environmental resources in developing countries can have severe consequences for self-sufficency, income distribution, and future growth potential in the developing world."[10] They have further clarified that, "Thought there is considerable dispute concerning the environmental costs associated with various economic activities, concensus is growing among development economists that environmental considerations should form and integral part of policy initiatives".[11]

Since man, nature and environment are indivisible, man must live maintaining full compatibility with nature and taking it as premise, we should develop our entire techno-economic structure. Due to this perception, India's wise men had emphasized upon the economising and optimum utilisation of the world's limited resources and they had looked upon nature as the mother.

(4) The concept of Integral Man in the form of all pervading *Brahma*

Western economics assumes the concept of 'economic man' whose decisions are based entirely on the calculations of gain and loss, in terms of materialistic wealth. The capitalistic system considers a man as a mere selfish being lingering after money, whereas the communist system considers him a feeble lifeless cog in the whole scheme of things. But the Bharatiya Approach completely rejects this concept of economic man and in place of it introduces the concept of 'Integral man'. Indian thinkers have not looked upon man merely as a gross physical unit, working like an insensate machine to satisfy his biological and materialistic needs; instead, they have contemplated him as a subtle and conscious living unit, working as an integral part of an all-pervading *Brahma*. According to them, every man is the embodiment of what is known as *Brahma*. In the words of Dr. V.K.R.V. Rao

"Human being is more than a mixture of mind and matter. He has a soul, if you prefer a conscience. He has values. He possesses a force which is greater than any other force in the world which our sages called the 'soul force'."[12]

Indian thinkers have assumed man as a combination of body, mind, intellect and soul (*shareera*, *mana*, *buddhi* and *aatma*). According to this thought-tradition, man is not only a mixture of body and intellect but it has the power of soul also which is pure, benevolent and divine. So, whereas man, because of the weaknesses, infirmities and selfish tendencies of his mind and heart, creates various problems for the society, he can also be an instrument in providing many happy and healthy solutions to the ills of the society and be an agent in achieving things conducive to the good of all provided an attempt is made to evolve the divine in him and to bring out his innate goodness to the fore.

In the present system, man, the higher creation of God, is losing his own identity. Instead of becoming the centre of the system he is becoming the servant of the system. Hence we have to create a system to which we can re-establish him in his rightful position bringing him the realization of his greatness, reawaken his abilities and encourage him to exert himself for attaining divine heights of his latent personality. Since the concepts like 'economic man', 'scientific man', 'biological entity', 'social animal' etc, have all proved to be inadequate and irrelevant, the Hindu concept of 'integral man' should form the basis of our future plans. Thus in Bharatiya Approach man is more than an economic being. Economic problems have their legitimacy but not supremacy.

(5) Integrated - Holistic Approach

The assumption of integrated rationality in the Bharatiya philosophy believes in an integrated, holistic and balanced approach. According to this approach, that economic system will be regarded as the best in which proper balance between *vyasti* (the individual) and *samisti* (the society) can be maintained. Freedom and individual interest can be allowed in the economic sphere but it should simultaneously be guided and regulated by moral principles and legal provisions in accordance with general public interest. Thus our system should be one which has room in it for both for private enterprises and for social control.

As already mentioned, Indian thinkers believed in the concept of 'integral man' (*Ekatma manav*) rather than in the 'economic man'. They have centered their philosophy on the conception of a man who is not motivated simply by wealth or economic factors only but is influenced by the sum total of various economic, social, ethical, religious, political, biological and environmental factors.

Thus, the Bharatiya Approach does not diagnose man's different problems, economic or otherwise, as unrelated to and isolated from each other. It looks at man as integrated organic whole and not as unrelated separate parts in the context of his diverse wants and problems. All the problems of man have a combined and total effect on his bearing and his existence, and so no one particular problem can find its solution in isolation. Man's multifarious problems are in fact inter-connected, inter-dependent and inter-woven. They act and react upon each other. This view is completely endorsed by Prof. Myrdal when he says: "...in reality, there are no economic, sociological or psychological problems, problems are just as problems, and they are all complex."[13] So no problems, be it as big an economic one, can be subjected to enquiry in isolation and no satisfactory solution to the problem can be offered in separation from the totality. Thus maintaining a panoramic view of life we cannot see economic problems merely in their narrow economic and financial terms and considerations, but relating to the entire social set-up we should try to find out their solutions on a broader ground. Hence the institutions to be evolved and the rules and regulations to be framed should not be unilateral or one-sided but all-round, universal and all embracing. We have to synthesize the economic, social, political, religious factors and considerations and it is also possible that some of our specialists who specialize only in one branch of life fail to grasp the full significance of this approach. Economic rationality is one of the prominent assumptions about human behaviour in modern economics. For example, it is assumed that a consumer will prefer that commodity or set of commodities from which he can derive the maximum utility. A producer will always select the least cost combination or he will produce aiming at maximum monetary profit and a factor of production will always strive to gain maximum remuneration. In short, through the assumption of economic rationality, generally economic factors are taken as the main variables in guiding and regulating human behaviour in the economy assuming other factors to be constant.

In a way, the concept of economic man in the form of the assumption of economic rationality enters in the area of economic thought. But in the real world, this assumption is not correct in the context of human behaviour. Ancient Indian thinkers had very well understood this very fact. According to them, besides economic variables, human behaviour has much to do with human endowments, social attitudes, political and legal arrangements, motivations, moral, religious and cultural factors, social customs and traditions, value system and many other such factors. So in their opinion, economic facts cannot be studied in isolation to other social facts and an analysis in 'economic terms', abstracting from the social matrix cannot produce valid and useful results. Therefore, it is essential to have an integrated approach while analyzing human behaviour in the day to day life.

Prof. Myrdal too seems to agree with this view when he says that:

"Human behaviour is not constant like the movement of celestial bodies or molecules. It is dependent upon, and determined by the complex living conditions, the institutions, in which people exist, and by their attitudes, as those have been moulded by, at the same time as they are reacting against, those living conditions and institutions."[14]

Now, many economists of the world seem to be supporters of this view. Therefore, today it is necessary that we should make the assumption of integrated rationality as our base instead of economic rationality to keep our analysis a practical one. We have to develop such a system in which man can be encouraged and motivated to accommodate his individual interest in tune with the social interest and thus optimum social welfare can be achieved.

Indian intellectuals were the supporters of class-cooperation and class-complementarities, not of class struggle. They had this basic belief that for the development of the whole society, each class is essential and useful. They were not in favour of sacrificing the interest of one group for promoting that of another. Rather they tried to create a harmony between the diverse elements of the society. In this effort it is but natural to pay more attention to the weaker sections of the society in order to develop a just and an egalitarian society. Thus in the light of ancient Indian thought we should make an attempt to evolve a social structure in which a proper balance could be struck between wealth and *dharma*, materialism and spiritualism, accumulation and renunciation, earning and distribution, here and hereafter, personal and public interest, freedom and control and all such things.

(6) Dharma (or morality)–based economic structure and Development Model

In the Indian tradition of thought *dharma*, *artha*, *kama* and *Moksha* have been considered four principle aims (i.e. *purusartha chatustaya*) of life. According to it, all the activities related to earning and consumption should be conducted on the basis of *dharma* in such a way so that it would lead to *Moksha*. Therefore, in the concept of *Mangal* development the stress will be on *dharma*-based economic thinking in place of capital and market based economic thinking and also on human-centred thinking rather than commodity-centred thinking. The focus will be on both prosperity as well as morality (*sadachar*). Thus the *Mangal* development will try to establish *dharma*-based economic structure.

It is beyond doubt that Indian society, Indian thought and Indian mind and psyche are basically '*dharma pradhaan*'. Here the essence of 'Dharma' is not in the dogmas and creeds, in the rites and ceremonies which repel many of us, but in the principles which have to observed in our daily life and social relations. The word '*dharma*' is derived from the root '*dhr*' (to uphold, to sustain, to nourish). It clearly shows that the concept of *dharma* brings the forms and activities, which shape, sustain and nourish human life '*Dharnad dharmamiti-a-hur dharmana vidhrtah prajah*'. In this context *dharma* becomes the set of moral and social rules and regulations, which are essential for the smooth working and balanced growth of the society. In this way *dharma* and morality become synonymous. According to them, morality or *dharma* cannot and should not be separated from economics, economic laws, economic doctrines and economic behaviours. As Aiyangar puts it, "The interdependence of economics and ethics has been a fundamental assumption of all Indian thought."[15]

While endorsing this view, Gandhiji observed, "I must confess that I do not draw a sharp or any distinction between economics and ethics. Economics that hurts the moral wellbeing of an individual or a nation is immoral, and therefore, sinful."[16]

Dr. VKRV Rao also observes:

"What seems to be is that the world cannot afford this imbalance between ethical and economic development whether in the traditional or in the industrial societies and that what we need is right balance between ethics and economics. What Vinobha Bhave would call integration of science with spirituality or what may otherwise be termed as the integration of economic development with spiritual values."[17]

Among the modern economists, Prof. Myrdal has also declared that "economics is a moral science"[18]

Not only that, just two days before his death even Pt. Jawahar Lal Nehru himself wrote from the circuit House at Dehradun the foreword for the well-known Gandhian thinker Sriman Narayan's book *Socialism in India*. He says

"In India it is important for us to profit by modern technical processes and increase our production both in agriculture and industry. But in doing so, we must not forget that the essential objective to be aimed at, is the quality of the individual and the concept of Dharma underlying it."[19]

Indian sages have always regarded that the world is under moral law, that the life is the scene of man's moral choice. It is *dharmakshetra*. Perhaps on this belief Indian thinkers have declared *dharma* or morality as the basis of economics. However this does not mean that we are negating the importance of wealth. What we want to emphasize is that wealth alone can not provide the fullest and highest satisfaction in life; though major and very significant, it is a part of life and not the whole. It is a means not an end in itself. It is but one of the four principles of life (i.e. four *purusarthas* – *Dharma, Artha, Kama, Moksha*).

Thus we are the hard believers in a happy and healthy blending of ethics and economics. If at any time, there arises a conflict between the laws of ethics and the laws of economics, the laws of ethics must undoubtedly be preferred and observed. In this context, Kautilya, Yajnavalkya and Narad have unequivocally declared that –'*Arthashastrastu Balvad Dharmashastramiti Sthitih*'[20]. That is why in Indian thought wealth (*Artha*) has been given second place to ethics or *dharma*. The fact that *Artha* comes after *Dharma* in the sequence of the four *purusharthas* is proof of this. In the *Shantiparva* of *Mahabharata*, Nakul and Sahadev while expounding the fine balance between wealth and ethics (*Artha and Dharma*) said that it is only wealth blended with *Dharma* (ethics) and *Dharma* (ethics) blended with wealth can only give good results in this world. In this way, Indian thought repudiates Adam Smith's idea that Economics is the science of wealth. It defines economics as the science of ethical economic principles.

Thus, in the socio-economic structure of our dream, '*Artha*' is secondary to '*Dharma*' and economics is the handmaid of ethics. According to *Bharatiya* values of life, even after accepting the importance of *artha* and *kaama* it is always stressed that they should always be controlled, regulated and guided by *dharma* (moral laws) and they should also be used for *dharma* (i.e. social interest). Whenever these moral laws were violated it resulted in the downfall of the society. Probably being perturbed at such a situation Vyasji was constrained to say, 'I am crying with raised hands that Artha and kaama should be followed according to dharma but no one listens to me.' (*Urdhvabahuviromyesh nahi Kashchitsrunoti Maam-Dharmaadarthashchakaamashcha sa Dharmam kim na Sevyate.*)[21] The same thing has been explained by Gandhiji in these words :

"True economics never militates against the highest ethical standards, just as all true ethics worth its name must at the same time be also good economics. An economics that inculcates mammon worship and enables the strong to amass wealth at the expense of the weak is a false and dismal science."[22]

To give practical shape to this approach ancient Indian social philosophers created an institutional set-up and a value system so that it might become a routine way of life to act and behave in accordance with moral principles and social ideals. With this in view we can see the role and importance of various Hindu institutions, concepts and values of life, e.g. the four *purushaarthas*, *varnaashrama*, joint family system, *gurukula* system of education, *panchmahayajnas* and other *yajnas*, *daana dakshina*, *istapurta*, concept of omnipresent *Brahma*, trusteeship, virtues like compassion and philanthropy and the spirit of love, cooperation, purity, fellow-feeling, renunciation and welfare of all etc. Besides this we also find the concepts of just price, just interest, just wages and just distribution in the ancient Indian literature which can serve as a guide to develop alternative systems.

It was the duty of *smritikaaras* in ancient India to suggest changes in various socio-economic institutions and concepts according to the requirements of the society and according to time and circumstances. In order to implement and vitalize the moral and humanitarian values of life in economic field, today, it is of paramount importance that new institutions be organized and developed, old values be reinterpreted, explained and if necessary be discarded in tune with the changing times and circumstances, and new outlooks and values be established and inculcated in the context of present-day needs.

Thus the *Bharatiya* Approach reminds us of those social and moral values on the basis of which a new socio-economic structure can be built in tune with the spirit of time. According to it sacrifice and not acquisitiveness, service and not selfishness, renunciation and not accumulation, nourishment and not exploitation, cooperation and not conflict, love and not hatred, trusteeship and not absolute individual ownership over the means of production should from the basis of the new socio-economic order.

Recently, many experts have begun to calling for a new value based approach to development. Traditionally, indicators of development have encompassed mostly social and economic measurements, household income, educational level, infant mortality rates, and so on. The Bahai International Community has propossed to the World Bank a set of guidelines for applying spiritually based criteria to the measurement of development. At the heart of this conception is the understanding that human nature is fundamentally spiritual and that spiritual principles provide an enormous motivational power for bringing about postive social change. In this regard it has suggested five universal spiritual-moral principles : (i) Unity in diverssity: (ii) equity and justice; (iii) equality of the sexes; (iv) trustworthiness and moral leadership: and (v) independent investigation of truth. These five principles should further be applied to following five policy areas : (i) economic development; (ii) education; (iii) environmental stewardship. (iv) meeting basic needs in food, mutrition, health and shelter; and (v) governance and participation.[23] Dr. V.R. Panchamukhi's observations are also worth noting, "we should also remember that the global society is today facing unprecedented value-crisis, in addition to the other various types of crisis situations. Erosion of values in all walks of life has been one of the root causes for frustration of the development process. The values of contentment, cooperation, dutifulness, caring for others, sustainable consumption, simple life style etc. need to be resurrected in our midst."[24] In order to evolve national ethics Acharya Mahapragya and A.P.J. Abdul Kalam have proposed the following algorithim :

"A nation has to have ethics in all its tasks for sustained economic prosperity and peace.

If a nation is to have ethics, society has to promote ethics and value systems.

If society is to have ethics and value systems, families should adhere to ethics and value systems.

If families have to evolve with ethics and value systems, parenthood should have inbuilt ethics.

Parental ethics come from great learning, value-based education and creation of clean environment that leads to righteousness in the heart."

According to them

"There is a beautiful connectivity between heart, character, nation and the world."[25]

***(7) Sumangalam* is a multi-dimentional and extremely broad concept.** It includes economic, social, cultural, religious, educational, political and all other dimensions in its ambit. Its scope is not limited to humans, but covers the whole living and material world and the entire nature and it also encompasses the present and future generations within itself. It is not restricted to dealing with short-term, momentary and present generation but it is the concept related to long-term, long lasting and future generation. It is not about just fulfilling a person's needs but has to do with the promotion of his welfare. Thus, *sumangalam* is a unique concept which is both multi-dimensional as well as having multiple meanings.

***(8) Sumangalam* accepts the principles of self-reliance and *swadeshi*.** The phrase 'country's own resources' is used to emphasize to build up a self-reliant economy based on the *Swadeshi* Model. The concept of *swadeshi* is primarily a concept of awakening the 'self' of the society. It should also be understood clearly that *swadeshi* is not a narrow concept. Rather it is a universal and wider concept. There cannot be one single pattern of development for the whole of the world. Diversity is both a fact of life and beauty of the world. Because of this diversity, development patterns of different countries of the world would naturally be different. Every country or society can reach the maximum possible heights of *mangal* development only through its own development pattern based on its nature, temperament and environment. But it is also true that different countries should take advantage of each other's experiences and experiments while undertaking their development-voyages. Their mutual relations should not be in the nature of parasitic dependence. Rather they should be of interdependence, cooperation and complimentarity. At the same time this is also true that there are certain universal and eternal values of life which should be taken into account by all the countries and it is because of this that the *swadeshi* philosophy establishes itself as a philosophy of universal well-being.

(9) The term 'standard of life' used in this definition is wider than the commonly used term 'standard of living'. Standard of living is generally defined in terms of per capita availability of goods and services whereas standard of life includes many more things such as ideals and values of life-human, social and moral values, tension-free life, availability of pollution-free environment, spirit of love, affection, fellow-feeling and cooperation, self-respect and self-confidence, devotion etc. Thus the concept of standard of living exhibits merely the economic personality of an individual whereas the concept of standard of life expresses the total personality of an individual. The synonymous terms used in a *Bharatiya* tradition for standard of living and standard of life are the concepts of *bhavya* and *divya* or the concepts of *preya* and *sreya*. Kathopanishad (1.2.2) clearly describes that there are two different pathways, one is called shreya and the other preya. wise men thoroughly contemplate over both the paths. Those who choose shreya path, obtain bliss (salvation) and those who select the preya path, obtain worldly life of material pleasures. Thus, in our thought–process divyataa or *shreyas* has been given preference over *bhavyatha or preyas* and this has been the basis of our lifestyle as well. Through this very concept the present day world, intimidated by the mad rush for materialism, can find its own *mangal*-path.

Attacking the change in lifestyle caused by present wrong indices of development Kaka Kalelkar wrote in his famous book *Yuganukool Hindu Jiwan Drishti* :

"We have taken gentlemanness (*Bhadrata*), which was our innate quality, to the shops of clothes and shoes, taken it for a ride in motor cars and aeroplanes, and who knows where it will end up. Our *bhadrata* is today insulted by inexpensive cloths; it is injured if our homes are not decorated with foreign goods. The deposits against our name in the bank indicate nowadays our '*bhadrata*'. We have forgotten that lugging around this false sense of 'honour' on our heads and giving it undue respect is in reality a matter of great shame."[26]

Therefore, it is imperative to develop such a new lifestyle, which is not confined to the accumulation of expensive and unessential material objects but which can lead man towards a higher life.

Sumangalam is a philosophy which inspires man to move from animality to divinity and provides him with the framework necessary to move ahead in this direction.

A New Classification of Economies

The adoption of the concept of *Sumangalam* will make a sea change in the whole arena of development literature. Till now we have been classifying economies as developed, developing and undeveloped. However on the basis of the concept of *Sumangalam*, now the countries of the world can be classified as follows:

(i) Mangal Economy

(ii) Mangal–Oriented Economy

(iii) Mangal-less Economy

Other terms of the development literature must also be suitably modified as under: -

(i) Mangal-strategy

(ii) Mangal-Path

(iii) Mangal–Policy

(iv) Mangal-Model of Development

(v) Mangal Index

In reality, the word 'development' is incomplete till the word *mangal* gets attached to it. Therefore, we want *mangal*-development, not mere development. The term '*Mangal* Development' possesses so much capacity and completeness as if we have expressed our whole gamut of emotions and expressions though this one compounded word.

Mangal Indices or *Mangal* Measures

We have already discussed in our previous analysis that the indices of development based on Western development models are incomplete, Irrelevant and impractical. In fact, they are incorrect, deceptive and contradictory. Therefore, we must seek alternative measures and indices. We must also understand clearly that there cannot be a similar set of indices for all nations and for all times. In addition, it is not possible to give a totally quantitative measure of Mangal Development. Only some aspects can be quantitatively measured and that too to some extent but there are many other aspects which can only be experienced and which are related to realizations on an abstract plane. Taking into consideration all these issues, the *Mangal*- Development indices for India are given below. It must be noted that this is a primary draft and it is expected that necessary improvements and corrections will be made to it. These indices have been given, in spite of realizing these limitations. Here is a list of some indices that has been prepared just in order to indicate the direction of thought.

(i) Output per unit of capital

(ii) Output per unit of energy

(iii) Output per unit of natural resources

(iv) Employment Ratio– it can be calculated on the basis of the following formula : = Total number of employed persons/Total labour force

(v) Reduction in the number of zero-employment households.

(vi) Ratio of persons having basic necessities of life in the total population of the country

Or

Reduction in the number of below poverty-line households or households without basic necessities of life.

(vii) Reasonable equality in the distribution of income and resources

(viii) Reduction in income-gap and consumption–gap between the lowest 20 per cent and the highest 20 per cent households.

(ix) Equal opportunities to all for education and employment

(x) Pollution-free environment

(xi) Healthy life

(xii) Tension-free life- reduction in mental, domestic, social, occupational and international tensions.

(xiii) Happy and healthy sleeping

(xiv) Harmonious and happy family and community life.

(xv) Respectful place to women, children and aged persons in the society and proper arrangement for their nourishment and development.

(xvi) A feeling of love and cooperation.

(xvii) Availability of opportunity and facility for pursuing the higher ideals in life.

(xviii) Apart from humans, provision for conservation and nourishment of birds and animals

(xix) Freedom

(xx) Cultural progress

There is a growing voice in the world today calling for the replacement of the GDP based measurement and model for development. The Japanese economist Prof. Shigarotsuru has come up with the concept of 'Net National Welfare'. To arrive at the figure of this measure for a country, things like accidents, transportation problems, pollution, the declining level of social life etc. are subtracted from the GNP. The former monarch of Bhutan had stressed on the acceptance of the concept of 'Gross national happiness' in place of GDP.

India's former President, Dr. A.P.J. Abdul Kalam, while addressing young scientists in the Defence Research and Development Organisation, had said that we should measure our development in terms of the National Progress Index (NPI) instead of the GDP. This NPI should be determined by the minimum quality level of its citizen, the values derived from the legacy of civilization and India's uniqueness. He has further explained that the evaluation of this uniqueness can be evaluated by the promotion of joint family, feeling of cooperation in work, and choosing the right path in life. In fact, we should keep in mind all these ideas while coming up with the measures of *Mangal*-Development; this is rational and practical and absolutely essential too in today's world.

MANGAL-PATH (OR STRATEGY)

The *Mangal*-path is a three-fold path. There are three main paths to reach the goal of *mangal*-development- knowledge, work and devotion (*Jnyana*, *Karma* and *Bhakti*). These three paths are neither parallel nor opposite to each other; rather they are complementary and cooperative in taking one to the same goal. Only a good balance and proper combination of the three can take one to the goal.

In brief, devoted work based on knowledge is the key to *Mangal*- Development. That is why it is said that work without knowledge is blind and knowledge without work is lame.

Knowledge implies the education that helps to enhance one's intellect and skill, gives one a wide range of information, develops good qualities in one and gives direction to one's behaviour. It encompasses everything from general education to ethical, professional and technical knowledge. It is only through the study of various knowledge domains and sciences that the development of various ways, methods, and techniques for solving the diverse problems of life has taken place.

It is also the means through which society modifies its vision and perspective. As the level of knowledge of a society increases, the possibility of development of the society also increases.

Karma (work) is the concept that displays the utilization of the labour force of a nation. It indicates hard work and *Purusharth*. For development, it is imperative to make the best and right use of the entire labour-force of the society and it should not be allowed to go waste. In this regard, it is important to develop the right work-culture.

Bhakti (Devotion) means doing any work with the utmost concentration. When one does some work with a feeling of self-immersion and with utmost concentration, from experience we learn that one can produce more in the same amount of time and with the same amount of resources. This is precisely why Indian sages have stressed that one should work with full sense of devotion. This feeling prevents a person from dissipating his work-capacity and gives him extra energy for work.

FIVE STREAMS (*PANCHA PRAVAAHA*)

In order to implement the *Mangal*–Development model for India, there has to be a collective effort through five different streams :

(i) Intellectual stream – this includes all types of educational institutions and all academicians working in them, thinkers, writers, journalists etc.

(ii) Social workers- the activists involved in solving various societal problems through various projects.

(iii) Political activists

(iv) Spiritual Thinkers

(v) Bureaucrats

Abdul Kalam has also visualised a triangle comprising three streams of the society in order to implement his vision india 2020. He says, "Our job is to make the golden triangle of punyatmas (good souls who have sacrificed their own comforts for the benefit of the society), punyadhikaris (able persons in administration) and punyanetas (able and honest leaders) work countrywide, so that a lot of actions can be initiated and promoted at the grassroot level."[27]

Mangal Approach does not visualize a government-dependent or market-dependent economy. It believes in establishing a people-dependent economy or development through people's participation. Government will cooperate with people's movement. Hence, there is an urgent need to organize voluntary organizations comprising scientists, technologists, administrators, social scientists, social workers, rich philanthrophists, primary and secondary producers from rural and urban areas. Thus we want to establish a people–oriented, socio-economic order and want to develop a cooperative and participatory working pattern.

The Greater Role of Socio-cultural and Human Factors in the Process of Development

If man is not just an economic being, it implies that man can be motivated to work on planes other than economic. The experience of life tells us that only money can motivate a person to work to a certain extent, not beyond it. Man is ready to do even the work that he is not willing to do for money, or even greater work, for fulfilling his ideals or for reasons of ethics.

This implies that apart from monetary considerations, ethical and social factors can also play a significant role in motivating a person to get involved in productive work. This holds within it great possibilities and potentialities. Perhaps it is from this that the solution to limitation of resources for India's development can emerge. Till now in our development plan we have assumed the social, human and ethical factors to be constant and have only considered the development models based on financial investment. However experiences of 10 five year plans are witness to the fact that such models have not been successful.

Hence, after defining development as *Sumangalam*, we have to amend our approach towards determinants of development also. Factors of development are broadly classified into two groups- economic and non-economic. Though in development planning we do mention the importance of non-economic factors, yet in actual development process we neglect them. We assume them as constants while framing growth models. Now, it is high time to amend this approach and think over the following hypothesis.

Given the economic factors (i.e., material inputs) we can accelerate the process of development by mobilizing socio-cultural and human factors in a developing country like India.

A developing country like India has limited material resources, particularly capital. Foreign aid also cannot fill this gap fully and leave it without its negative effects. So, if these countries want rapid development then they have to search for some other way out. Here comes the role of socio-cultural and human factors in the process of development.

This is a new path which will provide a new approach and new type of growth models. In this regard I fully agree with Prof. Gunnar Myrdal, when he says,'It is my conviction that in twenty or even ten years time we shall have different approaches and use quite different concepts and theories from those we have been accustomed to using'.[28]

Prof. Myrdal has shown in his writings, the uselessness of some of the models, methods of approach and major concepts, which dominate the current literature on economic development, such as the frequent use of capital–output ratio, surplus labour and shadow prices.

Prof. A.K. Cairncross also seems to be in agreement with this approach when he says,

"Development is not governed in any country by economic forces alone and the more backward the more this is true. The key to development lies in men's minds, in the institutions in which their thinking finds expression and in the play of opportunity on ideas and institutions."[29]

As to how Japan developed first among the four major Asian countries (Indonesia, India, China and Japan) or how new values appear in a traditional society, and things like that, we need an analytical model with an inter-disciplinary approach, encompassing all aspects of the behaviour of a society, and not merely the economic.

Attacking the current belief that capital is the main force behind development Prof. P.T. Baur writes:

"Capital resources, which are often thought to be crucial, are usually less important. Moreover their supply and productivity depend on personal faculties, motivations and social and political arrangements. These resources are thus primarily an effect, a result, a dependent variable in the process of development rather than a cause or an independent variable."[30]

He further explains, "The significance of the determinants of material progress has been underrated, or even ignored, in most of the development literature. These influences have either been ignored altogether or have been treated pragmatically at best. Various reasons may account for this comparative neglect. These deteminants are not among the familiar variables of economic analysis are not really quantifiable; and they cannot easily be manipulated by official policy. But while these considerations may account for the redative neglect of these determinants of development, they do not affect their significance."[31]

In this regard prof. Kaushik Basu's observation is also worth noting "One disservice to development that traditional economic theory has done is to place self-interest on a pedestal. One of the key propositions that Adam Smith had developed was that, if each individual in an economy pursued his or her self-interest Consumers maximising utility, entrepreneurs maximising profit—society would automatically achieve optimatily, with the "invisible hand" of the market doing the job.....Fortunately, modern research in economics and psychology is making it clear that our other human qualities, such as altruism, personal integrity, and appropriate social norms and institutions are vital for economic development."[32]

A number of other economists and experts are also in agreement with this approach.

Here, let me quote a few lines from our Second Five-year plan also, "It is no exaggeration to say that the most important single factor in promoting economic development is the community's readiness to develop and apply modern technology to the process of production."

All this amply prove the importance of social and human factors in development process.

The acceptance of this new approach to development may pose the problem of quantification i.e., to bring it to a manageable mathematical framework. It is correct that non-economic factors are not readily quantifiable and they can not easily be manipulated by official policy. In fact, these are the considerations, which account for the relative neglect of these determinants of development, but they do not affect their significance.

While highlighting this problem of quantification, Myrdal writes:

"......there may seem to be an obvious explanation that the factor abstracted from the economic analysis-attitudes, institutions, modes and levels of living and broadly culture- are so much more difficult to grasp in systematic analysis than are the so-called economic factors. They undoubtedly are. But it simply follows that the problem of underdevelopment, development and planning for development in south Asia are themselves exceedingly, difficult and that they have yet to be mastered. An artificial restriction of "reality" to that which is seemingly easier to grasp misses the central point. For in the south Asian countries the "economic" facts cannot be studied in isolation from social facts."[33]

We must also remember that sometimes the mountains of figures have either no meaning at all for analyzing economic reality in developing countries or an entirely different meaning so that it is sought to be imparted by them.

A purely mathematical growth model cannot be prepared on these lines and it does not suit our requirement. However, we can definitely prepare a broad analytical development model based on this approach. It requires a deep study and research in which Indian scholarship should accept the challenge and give a new direction to the whole world.

Now we can see the change in the approach of development economists also. According to Todaro and Smith "Development economics has a greater scope. In addition to being concerned with the efficient allocation of existing scarce (or idle) productive resources and with their sustained growth over time, it must also deal with the economic, social, political, and institutional mechanisms, both public and private, necessary to bring about rapid and large-scale improvements in levels of living for the masses."[34] Again they have said that :

"It is necessary to recognize from the outset that ethical or normative Value premises about what is or is not desirable are central features of the economic discipline in general and of development economics in particular. The very concepts of economic development and modernization represent implicit as well as explicit value premises about desirable goals for achieving what Mahatma Gandhi once called the realization of the human capital"[35]

Prof. Amartya Sen, has discussed capabilities approach of development. In his view income and wealth are not ends in themselves. He argues that the "capability to function" is what really matters for status as a poor or non poor person. According to him. "Economic growth can not be sensibley treated as an end in itself. Development has to be more concerned with enhancing the lives we lead and the freedoms we enjoy." According to him three core values of development are sustenance (ability to meet basic needs) self esteem (to be a person), and freedom from servitude (to be able to choose).[36]

Sen also maintained that the most important thematic deficiency of traditional development economics is its concentration on national product, aggregate inocme, and total supply of particular goods rather that on the "entitlements" of people and the "capabilities" that these entitlements generate. Entitlement refers to the set of alternative commodity bundles that a person can command in a society using the totality of rights and opportunities that he or she has. [37]

PARTNERS AND NOT FACTORS

Indian thought finds among diverse interests, not competition and struggle, but harmony. All should work in the spirit of harmony, in the spirit of making their contribution to a common good. 'Inputs' and 'Factors of Production' are the terms which do not find favour with the *Bharatiya* thought. For, these terms are too mechanical and smack of an exploitative spirit. We are participants and partners in a common venture. Labour is not just about hiring and firing. It is a precious partner. Indian thought believes in an economy in which we have use for one another's talents and contributions and not an economy where the vast masses and their talents become redundant by some impersonal, unknown market operations. This approach will lead us to an economic system in which everyman can work with dignity and self-respect and hope to get a legitimate share from the common pool.

The Central Direction-Gross Social Happiness (GSH)

Here the term happiness (*sukha*) has also been used in a special meaning. Happiness is a very broad concept related to body, mind, intellect and soul (*shareera*, *Mana*, *buddhi* and *aatma*) and it cannot be expressed merely in terms of economic utilities. It is an experienced fact that mere materialistic and economic goods cannot provide happiness to man i.e., wealth and happiness do not always result in positive co-relations. However, it is also equally correct that man cannot remain happy without having access to the economic resources required for the satisfaction of the basic physical and material needs. Hence on the one hand we will have to make available all the necessary goods and services to a man which are required for his existence and for the fulfillment of his social and domestic obligations, and on the other hand, we should also make provisions for the satisfaction of his mind, intellect and soul. For this, we have to evolve and provide the necessary philosophy, worldview, approach, values, ideals, life styles and a set of social and human relations. This alone will bring the real happiness to the mankind. During this process we have also to keep in mind that it should raise the level of happiness of every individual living in the country. It indicates the egalitarian approach or development with social justice.

Now people are seriously thinking to disown GDP based mindless growth model which does not make people happy. GDP is a crude measure that counts many social negatives as positive (incarceration etc.). It also fails to count services that enhance social wellbeing (parents caring for children, etc.), degradation of critical assets (forests, water, air, etc.) and intangible factors such as happiness (the utlimate goal of many people).[38] Therefore many thinkers of the world are accepting that the purpose of life itself is a pursuit of happiness. And mere material prosperity need not bring happiness always. According to the calculation given by a British based agency, in terms of Gross National Happiness India has beaten many of the rich countries of the world. India ranks fourth in the table of happiest populations in the world with 34 percent of its inhabitants being very happy whereas on a global scale, only 20 percent of people claimed to be happy. Recently Adrian while, the social psychologist has also shown in his world map of happiness covering 178 countries that people living in close contact with the environment were found to be happier. Similarly a recent report in the New Scientist stated that 10 happiest nations were all from Third world. Most rural cultures still have a strong identity, supportive communities, believe in reciprocity and adhere to a philosophy rooted in spiritual well being with little concept of accumulating material wealth.[39] This means that beyond wealth and material richness, there is something that make people happy.

Emphasising the need to accept happiness as the goal of growth madhav Mehra (The Founder President, World Council for Corporate Governance, U.K.) observes, "Is GDP growth the ultimate satisfier of human specie? Richard Layard of the London School of Economics and the UK's House of Lords produced an elegant, brief and influential exposition of the new doctrine two years ago (i.e. in 1907). He argues happiness is the sole goal of human activity. Second, happiness is measurable. Third, we know what makes people happy and unhappy. Finally, policy should aim at achieving the greatest happiness."[40]

Keeping happiness as the central theme, the Fourth king of Bhutan, Jigme Singya Wangchuck has developed the concept of Gross National Happiness (GNH) which we have already referred.[41] Three concept of GNH is based on four pillars: (i) Sustainable and equitable socio economic development, (ii) Environemental conservation, (iii) Preservation and promotion of culture, and (iv) Good governance. Actually, Bhutan's king has began to speak about a specific Bhutan's path to development in pursuit of values that were consonant with Bhutan's culture, institution and spiritual values, rather than values that were defined by factors external to Bhutanese society and cuture.[42] The first international seminar on GNH was held in January 2001 in Zeist (Netherland) followed by second conference in February 2004 in Thimpu (Bhutan).

Now around the world there is a growing awareness that in order to build a peaceful, equitable and sustainable future, we must rethink the very foundations of our current economic system. The concept of GNH derives its inspiration from Buddhist Philosophy. Human happiness and wellbeing of the whole is a very Buddhist ideal. Buddhism puts spiritual and philosophical wellbeing alongside material wellbeing and includes our realtionship with nature itself. Material well-being clearly contributes to happiness, yet we are all aware that a state of happiness lies much deeper. Paradoxically happiness actually lies deeper than many of the important social and non-material considerations that are excluded by conventional economics and embaced by GNH. Ultimately, happiness is a matter of perception; a state of mind; a fact that is fully acknowledged by Buddhism and other world faiths. Gross National Happiness is a magnificient ethic. The substitution of a single word, 'happiness' for the word 'product' inject humanity, in all its rich complexity, into economics. Many tenets of economic orthodoxy are challenged, most obviously the assupmtion that increasing material wealth automatically equates with increasing levels of human happiness.[43] The case of Bhutan also underlines the fact that happiness can not be purchased from markets and it can not be equated only with material attainments. Bhutan has a GDP of just 500 million dollars. But it is one of the happiest society in the world and it has acquired this status on the basis of its own concept of GNH. While penetrating the question 'who is developed?' Tracy Worcester[44] has quoted a brainstorming piece from Dalai Lama showing the paradox of our life today. It is given below.

Who is Developed?

The paradox our age-Dalai Lama

We have bigger houses but smaller families
More Conveniences, but less time.
More knowledge but less judgement
More experts but more problems
More medicine,but less healthiness

We've been all the way to the moon and back, but have trouble crossing the street to meet a new neighbour

We build more computers to hold more informatin to produce more copies than ever, but have less communication

We have become long on quantity but short on quality

These are times of fast foods, but slow digestion

Tall men but short character

Steep profits but shallow relationships

It is a time when there is much in the window, but nothing in the room.

On this background of happines there arises a question- what should be the central direction of our concept of sumangalam? From our whole analysis of Sumangalam a new concept of "Gross Social Happiness' (GSH) emerges which takes into account all the quantitative and qualitative measures of mangal development mentioned above. This concept of Gross Social Happiness is undoubtedly wider than the concepts of Net National welfare, National Progress Index, Human Development Index, Quality of life, Gross National Happiness and the like. In today's world the aim of any socio-politico-economic system is said to be the greatest good of the greatest number of people. However, India conceives of something higher than this; it envisages welfare and happiness of all. (Sarvajan Hitaya Sarvajan Sukhaya-Welfare of all; or Sarve Bhawantu Sukhinah-May all be happy). In fact, according to Indian thought the central idea of an economic model is the welfare of all beings, not just humans; it proposes the welfare of all humans, living beings, animals and plants. (Sarva Bhoot Hite Ratah). This Central idea of happines and welfare of all it the core of Mangal Development. It menas that the concept of GSH will not be restricted to some particulare class or region, rather it will work towards the wellbeing of the entire society as well as of the universe. In this way, Mangal-Development will work towards and increase in the "Gross Social Happiness' and thus GSH will work as the Central direction of Sumangalam.

Long Term Socio-Economic Objectives:

On the background of Gross Social Hapiness, efforts will be made to achieve the following main objectives:

1. **Food for all;** It implies the guarantee for the fulfillment of basic requirements of life like food, clothing, shelter, drinking water and security etc for all the people.

2. **Health for all;** Stress will be laid on adherence to basic rules of health and to preventive methods (right food, exercise and conduct). In order to make health care accessible to all, stress will also be laid on *Ayurveda*. *Yoga-Pranayama* and nature cure.

3. **Education for all;** With this aim in mind, it is important to develop a system of education that is easily accessible, can inculcate values of good character and is useful for the society. There should be complete and equal opportunity for each child to develop his or her talent. The curricula and the model of education need an overhaul. It should be framed in accordance to our culture, nature, environment, situation and requirements.

4. **Employment for all;** Effort will be made to ensure appropriate work for each individual and

to find an appropriate person for each piece of work. At least one member of each family must be guaranteed full and gainful employment. With this end in mind, there is a need to take a new look at all our employment policies. Employment-generating production and investment policies have to be introduced. For this we have to adopt a model of employment–led growth strategy instead of growth-led employment strategy. It is also essential that industrialists give up anti-worker approach and workers should give due importance to work-culture. Above all, practical policies have to be designed in order to achieve the goal of a sustained development with social justice.

Now many prominent economists and social thinkers of the world have started realizing the significance of this moral and integrated approach for establishing a new and better socio-economic order and naturally their thinking is increasingly veering round the *Bharatiya* thought. In this respect, Dr. Schumacher ardently pleads for 'a technology with a human face' and a study of economics 'as if people matters'. According to Paul- Masc Henry, 'The new world order can only arise from an ethico-political negotiation.' A book published by the UNESCO Press entitled *Culture, Society and Economics for "a New World*, pleads for 'a new way of looking at things and the adoption of new habits and new attitudes to facilitate the advent of a more equitable system for a society as a whole."[45] Not only this, many scholars have now started to discuss about the 'spiritual quotient in development.'

In 1997 the noted business writer Robert Kuttner published a book titled "Everything for sale" which offered a comprehensive account of the dangers of market fundamentalism.

Some new books seek new kind of world economic order- "Further Wealth" by James Robertson; "For the Common Good" by Herman Daly and John Cobb; "One World Ready or Not" by william Greider; "No More Throw Away People" by Edgar Cahn- New Concepts and streams - "New Economics"; "Humanist Economics"; "Ecological Economics" etc.; Ethical investments; Socially responsible investments.[46]

In this sequence French president Nicolar Sarkozi has also recently said that the economic progress should be redefined and in this regard he is seeking the help of two renowned economists – Amritya Sen, and J. Stiglitz. He has said that people are usable to understand that how statistical data are showing constant rise in economic progress while problems are increasing in the day to day life of the people at large. Hence there is a need to bring gross national product closer to the true index of quality of life.

References

1. Pachauri, R.K., Times of India, January 1, 2009.
2. Panchmukhi, Dr. V.R., Fifty years of Development Struggle-Some Reflections, ICSSR Occasional Monograph Series, 2003, pp. 19 and 24.

3. A Shloka recited in daily morning prayer (Pratah Smarana)

4. Op. Cit.

5. Ramcharitmaanasa, Ayodhyaakanda, 253, 2.

6. Capra, Fritjof; The Turning Point

7. Yajurveda 36-10.

8. Yajurveda 36-17.

9. World Bank Atlas, 1997.

10. Todaro, Michael P. and Smith, Stephen C., 8th edition, 2007, p, 497.

11. Op. cit, p. 498.

12. Rao, Dr. V.K.R.V.; Value and Economic Development, p. 142.

13. Myrdal, Gunnar; Against the Stream, p. 142.

14. Myrdal, op. cit., p. 139.

15. Aiyangar, K.V. Rangaswami; Aspects of Ancient Indian Economic Thought, p. 22.

16. Prabhu, R.K. and Rao, U.R.; The Mind of Mahatma Gandhi, p. 152.

17. Rao. Dr. V.K.R.V.; op.cit., pp. 43-44.

18. Myrdal, Gunnar, op.cit., preface viii.

19. Nehru, Pt. Jawahar Lal, Forward (Socialism in India, Sriman Narayan's Book).

20. Kaut. III, 1; yaj.II.21; Naradsmriti, Introduction, 39.

21. Vyas, Bharat Savitri Strot, Quoted from Dharmaank of Kalyan, p. 144.

22. Gandhiji; Harizan, Sept. 10, 1937.

23. Gujral, Bani Dugal; Spiritual Quotient in Development, Times of India, 21, 11.2000.

24. Panchmukhi, Dr. V.R., Op.cit., p. 24.

25. Mahapragya, Acharya and Kalam, APJ Abdul; The Family and the Nation, 2008, p. 291.

26. Kalelkar, Kaka; Yuganukool Hindu Jiwan Drishti.

27. Kalam, APJ Abdul with Rajan, Y.S.; India 2020-A vision for the New Millennium, 1998, p. 275.

28. Myrdal, Gunnar; Asian Drama, Vol. I, Preface, p. XIII

29. Caincross, A.K.

30. Baur, P.T.; Dissent on Development, p. 76.

31. Baur, P.T.; Op. cit., p. 80; see also pp. 284 and 325.

32. Basu, Kaushik, Professor and Chairman, Department of Economics, Cornell University; Hindustan Times Sept. 12, 2009.

33. Myrdal, Gunnar, Asian Drama, Vol. I, p. 28.

34. Todaro and Smith; Op. cit, p. 43.

35. Todaro and Smith; Op. cit., p. 47.

36. Todaro and Smith; Op. cit., p. 51, 55-56; see also Sen, Amartya; Commodities and Capabilities, 1985; Development as Freedom, 1999.

37. Meier, Gerald M. and Rauch, James E., Leading Issues in Economic Development, 2007, p. 31; See

also Sen Amartya: 'Development-which Way Now?', Economic Journal, Dec. 1983; Poverty and Famines; An Essay on Entitlement and Deprivation, 1981; Choice, welfare and Measurement, 1982; "Poor, Relativity Speaking", Oxford Economic papers, July 1983; and Commodities and Capabilities, 1985.

38. Frank Dixon in Gross National Happiness and Development (ed. by) Karma Ura and Karma Galay, 2004, p. 105.

39. Op. cit., p. 128.

40. Mehra, Madhav; Dematerialising growth, The Tribune, June 11, 2009.

41. For detail regarding the Concept of 'Gross National Happiness' see a book entitled Gross National Happiness and Development edited by Karma Ura and Karma galay, Published by the Centre for Bhutan studies, 2004.

42. Op. cit., preface, viii.

43. Op. cit., pp. 77, 122, 128, 174, 175.

44. Op. cit., p. 128.

45. Narain, Sriman; Towards the Gandhian Plan, p. 7-8.

46. Rajni. Bakshi in the book Gross National Happiness and Development (ed. by op. cit.), pp. 202-210.

3

A *Mangal* Draft for Socio-Techniquo-Economic Structure

The creation of an appropriate socio-economic structure is the most important requirement for *Mangal*-Development of India We can achieve our goal only by creating a new structure keeping in view our own circumstances and being in tune with the present time. A preliminary proposal for this structure is presented below:

1. Environment friendly technology with human face:

It goes without saying that technology is an important and powerful thing. Technology is restricted to not just factories, production and economy but has a great impact on our social relationships, cultural consciousness, thoughts, ideas, sentiments, life values and our lifestyles as well. Hence it is imperative for any society to fully comprehend what kind of technology it employs. The moot point today is to decide whether we should go for Western technology or should we develop our own indigenous technology. In this regard, even the enlightened Western thinkers are now realizing the evil consequences and disastrous effects of this Western technology and are warning against it. The gloomy thoughts that sadden the Western mind are related to urbanization, energy crisis, pollution, the rapid exhaustion of natural resources, mechanization, the emptiness experienced in life in spite of ever growing use of consumer goods, and absence of peace and happiness. Currently prevalent so- called scientific rapid mechanistic technique and technology have made man a helpless, inanimate cog in a wheel; in fact in many areas man is now being considered redundant. It seems as if such technology first creates a problem and is then used up solving the same. Huge machines, gigantic factories, mega cities and indiscriminate use of non-renewable energy have given rise to many psychological, mental and physical problems, social unrest and crimes and ecological imbalances and much resources is now being used up simply to solve these very problems. Many Western scholars like Schumacher, Mishan, Gailbraith and others are the representatives of this kind of thinking and they tried to create environment-consciousness among the people. The present day technology is disrupting organic relationships, spreading poison, rapidly depleting the earth's non-renewable stock of scarce mineral and energy resources, degrading moral and intellectual qualities of man and breeding violence-violence against nature and violence against one's own fellowmen. Experience all over the world shows that the use of chemical fertilizers, pesticides and high yielding varieties of seeds is detrimental in the long run and is turning agriculture into an ever-lasting high cost economy pushing the small farmers out. The Uruguay Agreement has only made the situation worse and more dangerous, so that in the coming years farmers in countries like India are likely to be at the mercy of multi-national companies.

The modern Western technology is recommended because it is claimed (i) that it produces more and (ii) that it produces cheaper. We should deeply examine these two tall claims of Western technology before going for it. It has certain deceptive appearances but we must look beyond those appearances.

The system is conceived in huge proportions and it is always on the move and is turning out huge quantities of goods and commodities. There is no doubt therefore, that in a certain sense the system is productive. But this may not be the sense which is important to a citizen as a consumer. Here, it will be important to know about the system of circular production, which is the direct result of this Western technology. Production in this system is circular and self-consuming. It tends to pile up production figures without raising, at least, in the same ratio, living standards of the people. Things are produced (a lot of which never enter into the stream of consumption) but are used up in the self-maintenance of the system itself. Exchange values are created which never get converted into use-values. Coal produces iron and iron produces coal. It will be an interesting and direction-giving study if somebody selects 40-50 commodities, which are not directly consumption goods but, which are supposed eventually to produce them. Things like coal, iron, aluminum, steel, office space, office furniture, wood, good deal of transport, communication, power, metals, etc. Then find out by a sort of double entry reckoning system, how much they enter into the production and consumption of one another. I think it will then remove, to a large extent, our misconception that Western technology produces more.

The large-scale system of production, based on modern technology, also claims to produce things cheaper. This claim also requires deep enquiry. It will be interesting to compare in terms of their cost to the consumers the supply of such things as shoes, food, textiles, sugar, pottery, agricultural implements, medicines, etc as produced by big industrialists and as produced at a more modest technological level or/ and on a smaller scale by producers in villages and towns. If we take this type of study, then we may find it difficult to maintain that things produced by large-scale complicated machine-using industries are always cheaper. For instance, everybody knows that the shoes made by Bata are more expensive than shoes made by small operators. This conclusion is also true with regard to various other commodities, like agricultural implements, textiles, sugar, foods, oils, pottery, utensils, hosiery goods, radios, fans and many other engineering products. If it is true that the products of big, highly sophisticated industries are not always cheap than the products of handicrafts and small-sized and medium-sized industries, then we should go for a decentralized economy run by people without their command. In those cases where the advantages lie with the system of large-scale production, it will be good to know its extent.

Now, it is amply clear that it is neither desirable nor advisable to transfer wholesale Western technology. For it has been developed only to subserve the ends of centralized large scale industries and urbanized societies only. As such, it has brought into existence an economy that is based both on exploitation and an ever-widening gulf between the haves and have nots in different spheres. Moreover, many studies have shown that these technologies are not even cost efficient, labour efficient or capital efficient. In fact, they cause large scale wastage of resources and that is why in the last 200 years 20 per cent of the world's population has already used up three-fourths of the world's natural resources.

Under the above circumstances, the moot question is what kind of technology we should develop and use? In this context the concept of 'appropriate technology' is interesting. This concept was first coined and popularized by Prof. Schumacher in the early 1960s. The success of any alternative strategy for development depends on the deployment of an appropriate technology. Therefore we must clearly understand the significance and dimensions of this concept of appropriate technology. In the Delhi meet of the UNIDO in 1978, appropriate technology was defined as follows:

"The concept of appropriate technology was viewed as being the technology mix contributing most economic, social and environmental objectives in relation to resources, endowments and conditions of application in each country. Appropriate technology stressed as being a dynamic and flexible concept, which must be responsive to varying conditions and changing situations in different countries."[1]

Hence it is clear that the concept of appropriate technology is a dynamic and relative concept that takes into consideration a country's specific development goals, its special needs and socio-economic conditions and the resources at its disposal. That is why there cannot be one single appropriate technology for all nations, for all times, and for all circumstances. A technology that is appropriate for one nation may be inappropriate for another. A technology that is appropriate at a particular period of time may not be appropriate at another period. Therefore, the choice of an appropriate technology depends on a nation, its needs and its circumstance.

There is an inherent danger of this definition that 'appropriate' can mean various things to various people. If one is asked, which technology is appropriate, the answer may not simply depend on the situations of time and place, but also on one's vested interests, approach and values of life. Prof. Schumacher in his famous book "Small is Beautifull" had answered this question of appropriate technology. According to him for most countries, an appropriate technology can be found among those intermediary techniques which are cost-effective and energy-efficient, which is small scale, increases employment opportunities, which can be scaled up to provide people with work near the place of residence, which can be created, operated and maintained indigenously without the help of external capital and skill, and which produces goods and services mostly for local consumption needs by using indigenous resources.

This is precisely the reason why technologies appropriate for rich nations usually cannot be termed appropriate for developing nations. The appropriate technology is thus used to vary from nation to nation according to the capacities, resources and priorities of a nation.

Appropriate technology refers not just to 'hardware' like machines, equipment, financial arrangements, management system, sales arrangements for social infrastructural capital etc. It is also important to note that the choice of an appropriate technology means choosing not only the production processes but also choosing the production.

Criteria for choosing an appropriate technology:

For a developing nation like India, an appropriate technology should be such that:

(i) it should foster pleasure-generating production and healthy consumption while at the same time maintain people's autonomy.

(ii) it should be suitable to India's distinctive nature, needs and requirements, ethos and value systems, solve the existing problems in a reasonable manner and time, and be in tune with the socio-economic conditions prevailing in the country.

(iii) it should be able to produce mass consumption goods for the common man instead of increasing the luxurious goods for a selected few; it should be able to help in curbing the tendency of dehumanization of man and help him strive for higher ideals in life.

(iv) it should be capital and energy saving, labour intensive and at the same time efficient in terms of productivity.

(v) it should lead towards productive set-up.

(vi) it should be able to employ more of renewable energy sources than non-renewable.

(vii) it should be helpful in maintaining pollution-free environment.

(viii) it should help in reducing economic disparities.

(ix) it should be able to utilize local resources, talent and skill and foster their development.

(x) it should provide opportunity, culture and environment conducive to the task of becoming better human beings.

(xi) it should be based on milking the mother nature and not exploiting her; seeking blessing from nature and not on conquering designs, having the spirit of friendship and not indulging in fighting.

In short, in the Indian situation the ideal and appropriate technology would be one which in per unit of output, maximizes employment but simultaneously minimizes capital requirements, production costs and energy inputs. The perfect technology must also not be dependent on imports, should be able to produce goods which have high export-potential, cause no damage to the environment, can use fully the human skills that we possess and is not too commercially risky. It should also be able to produce goods for the common people by utilizing local resources, manpower and skill.

In light of the above, the following things must be taken into consideration while developing an appropriate technology for India:

1. Product preference- such products should be manufactured that have widespread acceptance in society. Therefore the product should be to adapt to changing needs, tastes and preferences.

2. Technology- the plant, able machinery and production-process as far as possible, should also be competitive to large scale production with respect to both cost and quality.

3. Organization- ownership, finance and market system should be so organized and managed so that extra capital remains available at the lowest level and it should be further utilized for local development.

There has to be a proper balance of the above elements for any technology programme to succeed.

For instance, there may be technology available for cloth production, but unless there is ready acceptance of the kind of cloth produced by this process, this technology is of no use. Likewise, a technology cannot be employed unless there are appropriate organizations and entrepreneurs to use and own it.

The ADTA in India has chosen three fundamental areas keeping in view the above factors:

(a) The industrial activities that increase the cash flow in their areas. This includes cement, paper, cotton, spinning, jute spinning and weaving, wool spinning, improvements in the production processes of chemical fertilizers and mini sugar mills.

(b) Those businesses which can be started by small industrialists with minimal capital investment. For instance, handicrafts, blacksmith's work, carpentry, edible oil business, rural utensils business, leatherwork and shoe making, rice mils, etc.

(c) Those techniques which can produce output for both the industry as well as for the household- for instance, rural transport, bio-gas, solar cooking equipment, animal husbandry, industries based on forest produce, improvements in small tractors, rural energy, rural sanitation, environment protection technologies, etc.

Whenever there is a need to develop technologies for poor people, it is essential to bear their needs, circumstances and means in mind. For instance, if we were to design appropriate housing for 75 per cent of the Indian population that lives in rural areas and small towns, we have to make use of such techniques that can use bricks of burnt clay, bamboo, twigs, locally available timber, etc. Cement, steel, iron girders, marble etc can probably be employed only for the houses of the other 25 per cent. Similarly, the loan process for poor people for buying bullock, ploughs, simple tools, fertilizers, seeds etc, should not be based on the modern banking techniques. Our modern banking process because of its inherent nature is more geared to lend out, say Rs. 1,000 to hundred people than Rs. 100 to thousand people. Hence it is required to develop a special banking process for poor people in rural areas that are cost-effective and simple.

In order to develop suitable technologies in India, we have to make efforts in two directions:

(i) Scaling up of Traditional Technologies

This area possesses a large potential for India's future development. In India there is a need to upgrade the traditional technologies in areas such as weaving, shoe manufacture, carpentry, blacksmith work, food oil extraction, utensil making, leather and leather goods manufacturing, grain processing and handicrafts. In this context, the upgradation of the technology used for utensil manufacturing in Khurja (Uttar Pradesh) is an important case study. Today the 'whiteware' utensils of Khurja are extremely popular both in India and abroad. Such successful experiments have also been made in Chinhat and Gaura (villages near Lucknow) and in Phulpur (near Allahabad). By a proper study of the cottage industries and handicraft manufacturing units located in the villages and small towns of India, there is a great scope for enhancing their productivity and efficiency by employing innovations based on new technologies. Khadi and the Village Industry Commission and certain individuals like Balasundaram in Coimbatore, Mohan Parikh in Surat, Manibhai Desai in Pune, Annasaheb Sahasrabuddha in Wardha and Nanaji Deshmukh in Gonda have carried out such successful experiments.

In this regard India's former President, Abdul Kalam's observation is also worth mentioning : "The presence of traditional Indian skills in medicine, metallurgy, construction, textiles, hydraulics or early shipbuilding was an integral part of our innovationess in ancient and medieva times."[2]

(ii) Adaptation of Modern Technologies to Indian Conditions

The modern technologies developed in other nations should be adapted according to our special requirements, circumstances and our resources. Directly employing foreign technology as it is can be a dangerous process. Therefore, we should adopt the concept of 'Technology adaptation' instead of 'Technology transfer'. Just as a surgeon first does a tissue matching before carrying out an organ transplant in human body, in the same way we must ensure that a foreign technology is suitable for our national body before accepting it.

Although some small steps have been taken in this direction, however a comprehensive and systematic process for this is still lacking. Our

Planning Commission and government are still in a dilemma. We are still not free from the temptation of simply employing a foreign technology as it is and this is precisely the reason why the development and implementation of appropriate technologies has not picked up momentum in India so far.

Instead of wasting our energy on questions like what kind of technology should be adopted or how much expenditure should be made on the development of technology, We have to first of all answer the question- technology for Whom? Apart from it, we have also to determine that the first and foremost need of our country is to improve the conditions of poor people. In this process, our direction regarding technology would automatically become clear. This question is closely linked with our approach towards life and our values. For this we have to change our value system. Only then we would be able to implement this programme effectively. When we talk about village-based small scale technology for India, this does not mean that appropriate technology for India in every sphere will necessarily be traditional small scale technology of cottage and small industries. India is such a wide and vast country that it is in itself just like a world. Here can be some spheres and occupations in which large scale capital-intensive technology may be more appropriate. For instance, for the production of many machines and equipments used in agriculture and small industries, we have to use large scale capital-intensive technology. The same is true for space science, information technology and atomic energy plants etc. Hence we have to move forward in a balanced manner so that we can raise the standard of life of the common people without foreign dependence (or with minimum possible foreign dependence).

Thus the need of the hour is to have a new development model or a new type of economy in which we can have integration between environment and development, Lester R. Brown has termed it as 'Eco-Economy', that is an environmentally sustainable economy. Till date more than 300 conventions and conferences have taken place to evolve a synthesis between environment and development. In this process many terms have emerged such as 'Alternative patterns of development and life styles', 'Eco-development', 'Environmentally Sound development', Development without destruction' etc. As a result of giving emphasis on environment, environmental economics and ecological economics have emerged. The ecological and environmental economics gives stress on interrelationship and interdependence of the biotic and abiotic factors of this planet.[3]

2. Decentralized Self-Reliant Economic Structure Based on Family of Villages

Gandhiji had spoken of '*Gram Swaraj*' and based on it, he envisaged every village to be made self-reliant. But today, new means of transport and communication have come up, and people's new and varied types of wants have emerged, in this situation for a single village to be self-sufficient or in otherwords to be able to produce all the goods of its requirement is rather impossible Therefore, by combining ten to fifteen villages, a new kind of structure of group of villages or family of villages will have to be formed to which I have termed '*Gram Sankul*'. This kind of '*Gram Sankul*s' should be formed taking into consideration issues of technology, natural resources, environment and others. We will have to make intense efforts so that '*Gram Sankul*' could become more or less self-reliant. In spite of that, every *Gram Sankul* cannot be completely self-reliant. In this situation, if one village-group is unable to produce an article of its requirement, it may procure it from the neighbouring village-group. In this way, there should be exchange of goods between neighbouring village-groups. If, even then they are unable to procure goods of their requirement, then they can procure it from far-flung village-groups. In this manner, the exchange process should operate between neighbouring to far-flung village-groups respectively. If the production of some articles is not possible and profitable in the domestic economy, then they can be procured form external markets. In this way, the entire economic set-up will have to be rebuilt on the basis of village-groups. This type of set-up involving local resources, local skills and local labour will go a long way in fulfilling most of the local needs. Moreover, this will reduce wastage of resources, minimize transportation costs, sustain the environment and provide avenues for employment.

Thus, we have to accept village community as the most important unit for the *Swadeshi* structure of development. A new development model will emerge from the efforts to be taken to make this unit self-reliant and independent. It will provide full opportunity to utilize indigenous initiative, skill and enterprise. Here it should also be kept in mind that one village community may differ form the other with regard to geographical conditions, climate, natural resources and people's attitudes. Hence, the form and format of their self-reliance may be different. New kinds of socio-economic relations will emerge out of this system. Thus, there is a need for rebuilding India's shattered economy and policy on the solid foundation of India's villages, rejuvenated and reorganized into self-governing units.

3. Adopting a Tri-sector Economic Model

Indian economy is not a mono-dimensional economy, instead there is diversity. This diversity is the source of our potential and richness. This fact has to be appreciated while framing new policies and plans. Indian Economy has been classified broadly into three groups: 1. Tribal Economy 2. Rural Economy and 3. Urban Economy. Therefore, we will have to make plans of *mangal*-development according to this tri-sector model of the economy. It is often the inability to appreciate the importance of the diversity of our economic foundations, which breeds the immature policy of converting villages and tribal regions into cities in the name of development. We tend to forget, that different regions have different set of resources, problems and requirements. Therefore, we must keep these factors in mind before proceeding forward. We should also not forget that fulfilling a particular requirement for all regions through similar articles is also not desirable. To explain it, I would like to give an example. We know that cleaning teeth is an essential condition for health. Because 'datuns' are not easily available in cities, hence it is understandable that city-dwellers have to depend upon toothpaste and toothbrush. But villagers are content with using *datuns* which is equally effective in maintaining oral hygiene. So how much is selling fashionable *toothpastes* and *toothbrushes* in India's villages by replacing the traditional *datun* in the name of modernity justified? After all, the objective is only to maintain oral hygiene. But we have created such a mentality and atmosphere, that availability and consumption of toothpaste has been established as a standard of development. Similarly, for the people who live in big cities, the consumption of carrots, radish, tomatoes kept in refrigerators in the name of salad is regarded as a high standard. On the other hand, a villager consuming fresh fruits, carrots and tomatoes by taking directly from his farm is labelled backward. Because of such misleading perspectives, we have been unable to differentiate the rural-urban distinctions in regard to water resources, means of production, house construction, consumption patterns, etc. So, these differences, due to diversity, have to be properly understood. Usually, the tribal population prefers to limit its wants and the village population tends to remain contended. Hence, it is both inappropriate and unscientific to have complete urbanization of all the economic regions. Therefore, for the full development and autonomy of all these three economies, we will have to devise long-term sustainable action-plans cautiously and efficiently. The order of preferences for all these three economies will differ.

In the set-up of **tribal economy**, we must give special care towards protection and proper utilization of all productive forests lands. Tribals must also be taught the use of their forest produce and methods and techniques should be developed by which their forest produce can become the source of their income and living.

In rural economy, rural industries, agriculture-based industries and diversifying of rural products should grow so that proper balance is maintained between food and non-food crops (i.e. cash crops) in accordance to the country's requirements. Care should also be taken so that animal husbandry and *panchgavya*-based production structure is strengthened.

In urban economy, we have to set up those industries which are pollution-free, based on new technology and useful for tribal and rural economies. Along with it suitable, marketing and financial institutions should also be developed.

For the transformation of the economy, Abdul kalam has suggested the creation of 7000 PURA (Providing Urban Amenities in Rural Areas) covering 6 lakh villages in different parts of India. According to him PURA envisage economic empowerment of a cluster of villages through the provision of physical connectivity, electronic connectivity and knowledge connectivity leading to economic connectivity. Based on the terrain and climatic conditions, there could be four types of PURA in our country- plain terrain, hill, coastal and desert. He further explains that, it is possible to get an insight of PURA by studying a few of the operational PURAs in different parts of the country, in Periyar (Tamil Nadu), Loni (Maharashtra), Chitrakoot (U.P.) and Byrraju (Andhra). [4]

Over and above, we have to formulate our whole structure and planning by maintaining proper balance between water, land, forest, creatures and people.

4. Reframing the Relationship between Agriculture, Small Enterprises, Large Industries and Service Sector.

Traditionally, Indian economy has been classified in another way also as: Agricultural sector or Primary sector, Industrial sector (which include small scale and large scale industries) and service Sector. After independence, we have disturbed the relationship between all these sectors consequent to pressures arising form Western developmental models. We have given central place to the large-scale industries in our economy and therefore they have been termed as 'basic and heavy industries'. Cottage and small-scale industries have been called as ancillary industries. These industries are primarily for cooperating and serving the large scale industries. Hence, they will have to operate on the terms and conditions, if not the largesse of the large-scale industries. Consequently, in India, cottage and small-scale industries have lost their autonomy and independence. Finally, the left over place in the economy has then been allotted to the agricultural sector. This became the order of preference while framing economic policies and allocating investment. Again, this Western developmental model has also taught us that to march on the path of progress, the place of agricultural sector in the occupational structure of the economy should progressively diminish while the place of industrial and service sectors should enhance. This has endangered the Indian agricultural and unorganized sectors, and consequently the nation has been rendered victim to the problems of unemployment, poverty, inequality and food security. Therefore today, it has become imperative to reframe the relationship between these sectors. *Mangal* development being integral in its approach is opposed to an 'either or' policy with regard to agriculture and industry. It believes in the complementarity and inter-relationship between agricultural, industrial and service sectors of the economy. But it defines this relationship in its own way which is radically different from the existing pattern. According to it, agriculture should be regarded the prime and basic activity in the economy. Around this prime activity should be built a structure of agro-industries and need-based cottage industries, the farmer or the local artisan, singly or in groups, converting his produce into consumption goods with the help of immensely improved and efficient small machines within the means of local finance. Thus, cottage and small scale sector should help, cooperate and serve the agricultural sector. On the one hand, it should manufacture tools and implements required for the agricultural sector and on the other hand it should produce consumption goods by utilizing the agricultural produce. Around this cluster of agro-industries should be built those heavy industries which are ancillary to the first and the second. There is a vast difference between this system in which agriculture and agro-based small industries are primary and heavy centralized industries ancillary, and the Western system (capitalist and communist both) in which heavy centralized industries are primary and small-scale consumption industries and agriculture are ancillary and incidental. This new order of preference has to be maintained and operated through the active cooperation of the service sector. In India, agriculture has always received this central position and hence, Indian economy is called agricultural economy. The development of agriculture used to be considered as a benchmark for overall progress. Therefore, in the *Mahabharata*, Narada asks Yudhistir about the state of the economy in these words:

"Are the agriculturalists content in your kingdom? Are there plenty of large ponds across the length and breadth of your country so that the farmer does not remain dependent upon rainfall? Are the agriculturists protected from damage to grains and seeds? Do you give them subsidized loan at the rate of 1%? Are the activities related to agriculture, animal husbandry and commerce performed by good and gentle citizens because the welfare of the people depends upon them?"[5]

This dialogue is of pivotal importance while framing our economic policies. Even in the verses of the *Rig Veda* we find importance attached to the issues of environment, forestry, animal husbandry, agricultural equipments, assessment of farming etc. (*Krishi sukta* and *Akshasukta*)

In the new contexts and contemporary age, India should seek to create and implement a viable cattle-based economy. King Nand of Gokul had over 9 lakh cows, while Vrishabhanu had 12 lakh cows. But our livestock population has continuously declined. After independence it declined more speedily. In 1951, for every 1000 humans, there were 430 cows, which have now reduced to 130. We should not forget that the cow represents the Indian identity.

5. Two-Tiered Strategy for *Mangal* Development

Mangal-Development in India would involve a strategy which runs simultaneously and parallely at two levels. The first level constitutes of the Indian population segment of around 15-20 crore people which is considered elite. We should select amongst them, those who are dedicated, skilled and conscious to their societal obligations and their talents. Their potential should be harnessed to attain excellence in diverse sectors and they should be supported in every possible way. Such talented persons in our society can meet the various challenges in diverse sectors by searching useful and appropriate technique and technology, rules and regulations, traditions and standards (*maandand*s) and can give a new direction to our existing policies.

The other level is constituted of the ordinary population segment of 80-90 crores. For these people class-wise and region-wise separate practical action-plans should be formulated. Their capability, potentialities, requirements and ground realties should be kept in mind while constituting policies for them. Any policy which ignores all these factors does more harm than good. We can understand this with the help of some examples. For instance, take the agricultural sector. We know that the size of land holding of 80 per cent of Indian farmers is just 1.6 hectares. Hence, in order to make these farmers self-sufficient, we require appropriate technological-know-how, agricultural methods and other essential policies apart form their efficient implementation. But without understanding this basic nature of our nation, we preferred blind imitation of the West and adopted the new agricultural technique based on high-yielding variety seeds and the increase in food grains output as a result of this technique was understood as a Green Revolution. Now, it is time for us to evaluate the results and effects of Green Revolution based on this new agricultural technique. Let us now discuss which parts of the country were blessed with the Green Revolution. We shall find that the Green Revolution was limited to Punjab, Haryana, western Uttar Pradesh only, and not in other regions. Why did it so happen? We are aware that in order to get high yields from these high-yielding seeds as compared to indigenous varieties, they require greater application of water, chemical fertilizers and insecticides. Hence, those parts of the country which did not have adequate water resources could not experience a Green Revolution. And what was the ultimate result even in those areas which experienced a Green Revolution? As a result of more use of water, in Punjab and Haryana, the groundwater levels have disturbingly gone down, and this has caused a water crisis. Excessive use of chemical fertilizers and insecticides has reduced the natural fertility of our soils, and has rendered large tracts of our farmlands barren. Also, the chemical content in food grains, fruits and vegetables has accentuated, and this is causing a host of diseases amongst its consumers. Another consequence is that the small farmer is unable to bear the cost of this new technology and is abandoning his land and running towards the city, while big companies buy these lands at throwaway prices form these farmers and are heading towards corporate farming. Farmers in greed for high yield take loans so that they can adopt this new technology but when the yield is less than expected, and when they are unable to pay the loans back, the only recourse remaining for them is to commit suicide. Such cases have been reported in the country. These new seeds are dangerously reducing the genetic diversity of native seeds, and the Indian farmer is slowly but surely becoming absolutely dependent on the hybrid seeds of international companies. This has created serious problems in regard to the food security of the country and safety and sovereignty of indigenous seeds. Therefore, there is need for immediate intervention by adopting effective policies. In this regard, keeping in consideration India's climate, soil, size of land-holding, resources and other requirements like seeds, fertilizer, agriculture implements, means of irrigation, appropriate sales and financial set-up should be developed and accordingly, our agricultural universities and agricultural research institutes should decide about the direction of their research, and then agricultural policy should follow it.

Similarly, a second example is about our livestock and milk production. Our dairy institutes have developed Jersey cows which provide 20-25 liters of milk, and on this basis tall claims were made in support of a so called 'White revolution'. Now, the milk of the Jersey Cow is known to be deficient in nutritious ingredients as compared to our local breeds. This also seems to be a conspiracy to destroy the genetic diversity of the Indian cow. Secondly, such hybrid species are out of the reach of poor farmers. Instead, we should have concentrated on doubling the milk output of our local breeds. This would have doubled the milk production and also allowed the common man to retain cows and buffaloes.

Hence, it is very much required that we should adopt India-centric perspective and approach in regard to the formulation and development of our entire research, technique and technology. Apart from it, we have a large number of small artisans and other skilled people in the country. By utilizing these people and their skill we should plan to start village-group level projects and works keeping in view the local resources and local needs. These projects should not rely too much on the government. Instead, they should be encouraged to become independent and self-reliant and the whole set-up of articles, market, finance, technique and technology should also be developed accordingly. A directory should be maintained for cottage and small-scale industries, both district-wise and trade-wise. For their protection and promotion, a support networking needs to be created. This networking will work both horizontally and vertically. Horizontal networking connotes, that small producers while producing similar type of articles, should work together and support each other in acquiring raw materials, brand, advertisement, technology training, financial help, etc. Vertical networking involves coordination between small entrepreneurs, customers and technical research institutes. In the prevalent situation, mutual understanding between the producers and workers regarding work-ethics is of utmost importance. The country can no longer afford to bear the burden of losses caused by strikes, lockouts and inter-union conflicts. Therefore it is essential, that industrialists change their anti-worker attitude and search for ways to make them partners in operation, decision and profit of the industries. In this regard we have to give practical shape to the concept of industry-family. On the other hand, workers should also think of adopting positive work culture which can enhance efficiency and increase production. Throughout the county, workers in different levels should be encouraged to adopt work culture, and promote those associated values and practices which provide incentive for work.

All in all, what we need is the implementation of a pragmatic policy which takes into account the Indian diversities, abilities, potentialities and possibilities and skills of its people. India has a large cultivable land (1200 lakh hectares), vast fertile plains of Ganga-Yamuna, wide river-water resources, availability of sunlight throughout the year, six seasons, rich bio diversity (approximately 85,000 types of plants), more than 3.5 million scientific and technical experts, (especially IT-based human resources), large source of (*ayurvedic*) herbal plants, a traditional technological expertise, *yoga* and *ayurveda*-based medicine and treatment, a big member of devotional, content, parsimonious (*mitavayi*) and industrious manpower, and rich societal-cultural traditions. In pursuing our policy of *Mangal* Development, we have to utilize this collective heritage of ours judiciously.

6. Employment -oriented Economical Production-process

The present production process is long, roundabout and extravagant (or uneconomical). In the beginning whatever amount of raw materials or minerals are used in the production-process, before reaching the consumers in the form of final products, a large potion of them is decelerated and used up. This production-process is largely dependent on machines and energy. Hence in order to operate it, iron in the form of machines and implements and coal for energy are required in a large quantity. This means that in this production – process in way coal is consumed by the iron and iron is consumed by coal, but the consumer does not get much out of this process. In this economic system there is unknown, indirect and distant relationship between the producer and the consumer. The producer knows the consumer by numbers and not by name, for instance, customers having 8, 10 or 12 numbers of shoes and *chappals* or customers having 30, 35, or 40 numbers of shirts and vests. In this type of system we can not imagine the live and organic relationships that can understand human sentiments and emotions between producers and consumers. Hence today's biggest challenge is to evolve a kind of production-process and mechanism which can produce the maximum with the minimum resources (or inputs) , which can have least possible deterioration of resources and which can develop humanitarian relationship between producers and consumers. Apart form it, we will have to give more stress on adopting that production technique which can increase employment and also that which can provide self-satisfaction to the working people.

7. Restrained and Ethical Consumption-Pattern and Lifestyle

The status, nature, direction and condition of an economy depends largely on its consumption-pattern. Therefore, it is necessary to understand the present ever-increasing consumption-pattern and the problems and challenges arising out of it. There are no two opinions about the fact that during the 20th century there has been an extraordinary increase in both consumption and in the range of consumer goods. By 1998 the world's total consumption had jumped to 24 trillion dollars which was 6 times higher than what it was 25 years ago. Globally 20 percent of the world's richest people account for 86 percent of total private consumption expenditure, the poorest 20 percent for only 1.3 percent. Worse, the gap between the rich and the poor is growing. In 1970, the ratio of consumption expenditure of the richest and the poorest people was 30:1, whereas in 1998 it become 74:1. Though even in India, the total consumption has increased, but its distribution has been totally on a wrong pattern. As a consequence of this, there has been a steady increase in the economic disparity in the society. Over a billion people in today's world have still no means to fulfill even their basic needs. It is certainly a cause for concern when deterioration of consumption resources, pollution of the environment and an excessive lust for luxury and conspicuous goods starts to deprive the common man from fulfilling even his basic needs.

The consumerist and ostentatious lifestyle, that we are steadily adopting today, are not sustainable in the long term, both from environmental and social perspectives. Not only that, this excessive consumerism is actually weakening the possibilities of practical and sustainable human development. The facts suggest that the consumers are stretching their income in buying more and more. Consequently, the savings of the families are diminishing and debts are increasing. It seems that a kind of vicious circle is emerging between consumerism, poverty, unemployment, illness, inequity and pollution. The growing global consumer market leading to aggressive-competitive advertisements, are giving rise to newer problems every day.

There is a mad competition to sell products through aggressive advertisements. An average American watches about 1, 50,000 advertisements on TV in his lifetime. According to an estimate, about 435 billion dollars are spent every year, worldwide, on advertisements. Such aggressive advertising is spreading rapidly even in India.

There is a race to make for oneself a special place in society through ostentatious consumerism driven by globalization of the consumer markets and aggressive advertising. This process has created a new class of goods called 'status goods' and new classes of people, different from the rest of the society, called 'global elites' 'global middle class' 'global teens' etc.

It is now being increasingly admitted that the main reasons behind the developmental problems and crisis is the defective consumption pattern and lifestyle. Therefore, in order to overcome the crisis and problems arising out of our present development model, there is a need to develop a more restrained and ethical consumption-pattern and lifestyle by making appropriate changes in our values of life and standards of social behaviour. It is a necessity to develop a lifestyle that is environment-friendly, that takes into consideration the interest of the poor, fosters cooperation, helps developing human potentialities, inculcates a feeling of social responsibility, takes care of the needs of not only the present but also future generations, and encourages creativity in individuals and communities. In the context of India, it is extremely important that even while raising our consumption levels, we do not ape consumerist lifestyle of the rich nations. In this model of consumption-pattern, care should be taken that the goods and services are available for providing the basic needs like food, clothing, shelter, education and healthcare to one and all. For this purpose it is necessary to give due attention to production of consumer goods for lower income groups, building low-cost housing, manufacturing of energy-saving devices, and development of inexpensive and safe storage facilities for food grains. Organic farming, the production and use of various types of bio-food, herbal products and chemical-free products must be encouraged. The consumers must also be given clear and comprehensive information about food and drinking products, medicines, health services, goods of domestic use and transport vehicle's safety etc. Multiple uses of products and a lifestyle that can help one to manage with a modest income and resources should be encouraged. The adoption of basic laws of health, restrain in food habits and behaviour, use of medicinal plants, Yoga, praanayam, ayurveda, indigirous treatment techniques and also re-establishing the role of family in social and day to day life will also help in the development of simple lifestyle. In this regard, it is important to do away with extravagance and make appropriate changes in clothing, decorations, house constructions, use of water, electricity and energy, weddings, functions, festivals, etc. The renound sociologist, Dr. Shyamacharan Dubey has described his conception of an alternative lifestyle in these words:

"The present lifestyle is tilted towards personal enjoyment, personal satisfaction, and personal consumption. This must change. In the new environment, there will definitely be a great feeling of pleasure and satisfaction, even when one foregoes some of his personal pleasures for the greater good of the society. The yardstick of success will no longer be what one has been able to do for oneself or one's family, but rather what benefit he has brought to the society, as a whole. An individual's success will be evaluated in the context of his social relevance and contribution in social welfare, and in such a society excessive consumerism will be looked down upon."[6]

Dr. Praful B. Desai, Director, Tata Memorial Centre, Bombay has once said that cancer is a disease we give ourselves by our lifestyle and habits and that 60 percent of cancers can be prevented by a prudent lifestyle.

The mechanistic worldview and its reflection in life-style, viz., materialistic way of life has had its inevitable adverse effects on individuals, societies and the environment. Western philosophy is responsible for a non-sustainable lifestyle, whereas the Eastern philosophy (especially Indian, Chinese and Japanese) is helpful in developing a pattern of sustainable lifestyle. Eastern philosophy has always maintained that universe is organic and holistic. All of them are unanimous that liberation from bondages is the ultimate goal of life (Moksha) and human body is a medium to to penance. These philosophies preach their followers to shun material pleasures as that is hinderance in reaching the goal of liberation.

Our ancient Hindu Literature is full of advice- 'check your consumption' or 'reduce your wants'. This was achieved in practice through subtle 'sanskaras' on mind. The intellect has been appealed to discriminate between good and bad, between desirable and undesirable, between shreya and Preya.

Just as the western philosophical tradition culminated in a mechanistic worldview and materialistic way of life, Indian philosophical tradition culminated in an organic, holistic and spiritual worldview and renunciative way of life. When people at large opt for a renunciative way of life their consumtion reduces. There emerges, thus, a pattern which is eco-friendly and sustainable. Hinduism is, thus, a plan of sustainable consumption and sustainable development.

In this regard Dr. M.M. Joshi[7] has unequivocally stated that "without restraint in consumption, without fundamental changes in consumption patterns and value systems the goal of sustainable development is simply not achievable." He is of the opinion that there is an urgency of developing a paradigm for 'sustainable consumption' on a global scale. According to him local and regional efforts to achieve sustainability are vital but have limited chances of success in the absence of a global consensus. He further warns "that unless the process of globalization is transformed by the spirit and values that inherent in the concept of 'sustainability', both in production and consumption, we shall be threatened by a devastating erosion of our ecological, social, economic, cultural and moral resources." That is why the suggests that, "scientists, engineers and health professonals should study and devise ways of transition to new models that provide increased human welfare with reduced consumption of energy and materials."

Acharya Mahapragya and APJ Abdul Kalam have also warned that "....without limiting or restricting desires through self restraint, both desire and wealth become dangerous."[8] They have further explained that "the main aim of the Indian Philosophy of economics was to take both the individual and the society towards peace and happiness. The doctrine of sukharthi samyato bhavet (a person during the period of happiness should be self-restrained) is significant."[9]

In order to bring about appropriate changes in the pattern of production and consumption, we have to pay attention to the development and use of technology that is appropriate for India. All in all, it is only by developing a pure, *satwik* and sustainable consumption pattern and lifestyle can our entire society overcome its present contradictions and move on the path of *Mangal*-Development.

8. Inter-Dependent Voluntary International Economic Relation and International Trade

One important question that arises is that what will be the approach and policy with regard to international economic relationships, international trade and globalization in the framework of *Mangal*-Development? Does it advocate a closed economy? In this context, one can say at the outset that India never had a supporter of closed economy in the past, nor will it ever do so in the future. However, we must understand clearly that the present international economic and trade relations are not based on a level playing field. One the one hand there are the extremely developed nations of the world, on the other are the poor nations. The affluent nations, while trading with their poor counterparts, impose their own conditions and exploit them both in export and import. In this way the poor nations are forced to become dependent on the rich nations in this process of international trade. Hence the present economic relations are mostly parasitic and exploitative or these are based on exploiter-exploityee relationships. In this structure, the poor nations are dependent on the rich while the rich exploit the poor nations in order to further their own development. We are not the supporters of such kind of relations. We desire a framework in which the nations have mutually dependent economic relations. They should carry out import and export on their own will, without anyone forcing them to, and international trade should be for the benefit of all. We support fair trade, not iniquitous. Before forging international trade relationships, India should carefully scrutinize the present international trade organizations and international events.

While looking from this point-of-view, it becomes clear that the efforts of the IMF, World Bank, WTO, and the multinational companies to bring about an economic reorganization in India, are driven by an external motive. Hence, fundamentally they are against India's own interests. The aforementioned organizations have not been created primarily for the benefit of India. Not only that, they have not been created even for the good of the entire humanity. In fact, they have been founded to serve the interests of a small section of the world.

Adoption of new economic policies in the name of globalization has neither significantly enhanced the level of the country's development nor increased employment. On the contrary, poverty, disparity and inflation have increased. There has been a negative impact on small-scale and agro-based industries. There has been a concerted effort to gain control of the natural resources and bio-diversity of India and infiltration of foreign goods in India's market and deculturization of families have increased.

In the name of disinvestment, the assets earned during the past 50 years, indigenous industries and their products have been given over to multi-national companies in haste and controversial manners. There is even a distinct danger to the nation's sovereignty as the patent laws are being amended against India's national interests under pressure from the WTO.

In the context of the WTO, it is important to act cautiously and frame appropriate polices and strategies keeping our long term interests in mind. It is important to have a nation-wide debate on important trade and economic issues, and a process of discussions with experts and specialists should begin. There should be discussions with other developing nations and a common forum should be formed in which India should step forward to provide leadership. In this respect an alliance should be forged with various nations intelligently.

Instead of falling in the trap of foreign investments and foreign trade, we should decide the nature, amount, area and conditions of such investments cautiously and intelligently, keeping our supreme national interest in mind. Policies that make our nation dependent on others can be suicidal. Ultimately foreign investment should be of benefit to us rather than simply making us dependent on them. They should make the national economy stronger rather than undermining it. Hence we should be able to make cautious and intelligent strategies in this regard.

In the present, it is not possible to completely ignore the WTO. Hence we must comprehend the mechanism and provisions of this organization and framework and understand its strengths and weaknesses, so that we can frame our policies skillfully and intelligently in order to safeguard our national interests. We must also form alliances with other nations to expose some of the internal contradictions of the WTO framework, which will ultimately help in bringing about a process of change in this framework.

We do not support a lop-sided and exploitative globalization. Rather, we are in favour of one that looks at the world as a big family and contributes to the welfare of the people. All in all, in the present geo-political and economic contexts, India must remain resolved and ready in its approach and strategies.

9. God's Ownership and a Caring Distribution Pattern (or Motherly Distribution Pattern)

One of the most important questions in any economic system is : who should the owner of the means of productions be? Capitalist economies maintain that there should be individual ownership over the means of production. In this way, individuals gain ownership over the means of production and they make all possible efforts to use this to further their own interests. History is witness to the fact that in such capitalistic countries people have to suffer due to conflicts, exploitation and inequality. Contrary to it, socialist nations have always advocated state ownership over the means of production. This is what they have termed as nationalization. According to them, the resources will be under the ownership of the state. When individual ownership is totally negated and absolute ownership of the state is accepted, the question of incentive and initiative raises its ugly head. The experiences of the socialist regimes reveal that one cannot be forced to work and produce to the optimum capacity under the threat of state authority. In this system, people are reduced to becoming the cogs of a production-machinery and their incentive and initiative for work are both finished off.

In this context Acharya Mahapragya an Abdul Kalam have also expressed the similar views. They say, "As a means of building an equitable, sustainable order, both the economic systems- socialistic and capitalistic-have not delivered. In our view, both socialistic and capitalistic systems are examples of extreme thinking. What is needed is a search for a middle path in which individual property is not banned completely and at the same time, there is no unrestricted or unscrupulous freedom for the accumulation of wealth. The crying need of the present age is the fixing of limits for both accumulation and individual ownership. The Cornerstone of Indian culture has to be, 'Do not amass inessential wealth and do not cause suffering to others in trying to achieve your happiness."[10]

In this context, the vital question arises that who should have the ownership rights over resources and production so that conflicts and exploitation can be avoided while at the same time incentive and initiative for work is maintained to the maximum possible level. In the light of Indian thinking and in the framework of *Mangal* Development, a novel notion of God's ownership is accepted. This means that neither the individual nor the state, rather god (i.e. society), should be regarded as the ultimate owner of the country's means of production.

Ancient Indian sages have time and again pointed to the teaching of the *Isho Upnishad(1) 'Ishawasyamidam sarvamyatkinchan jagatyam jagat tena tyaktena Bhunjitha ma grudhah kasyachiddhanam."* Tulsidas in the *Ramcharitmanas* has said, 'Know this universe to be pervaded by Ram'. *(siyarama maya sab jag jaani)*. Vinoba Bhave has said, '*Sabhi Bhumi gopal ki yaa men Atak kahan*' and Gandhiji has talked abut the principle of trusteeship. All this clearly express the unique idea of 'God's ownership'. According to this the ultimate ownership lies with God, whereas individuals have 'delegated ownership'. Therefore, in this system an individual will use his resources not simply for his own sake but will look upon these resources as a trustee. Accepting this concept, every individual can be inspired to produce to his optimum capacity, considering his work as a work of god and infusing in him a firm faith in God. Simultaneously, he may be prepared to take the minimum share only to satisfy his basic needs from the common pool and leave the rest for the use of the society. In such a society people inspired by this idea would present their entire earnings at the feet of society (or god) and out of it they would consume only a portion of it as *Yajan-prasada* or *yajana-shesha*.

This approach may appear to be impractical and strange to the people who are habitual of thinking only in terms of financial and economic considerations. But the people who understand the subtleties of human behaviour will definitely accept that the relation of man to wealth and property depends mainly on his attitude, and the change in attitude brings about the change in human behaviour also in that very direction.

Thus *'individualization of common property and the communalization of the individual property'* is the essence and the basis of the *Bharatiya* Approach with regard to ownership relations. This concept is undoubtedly superior to both the present day approaches prevalent in the capitalistic and communistic worlds. In the capitalistic system, the individual and private ownership is recognized in both the fields of production and distribution in such an unrestricted manner that it has become inconsistent or directly opposed to the interests of the society at large. In the process of liquidation of individual ownership and in its efforts for nationalization of industries, trades and means of production, the communistic society establishes absolute ownership of the state on everything that exists in the state form man to atom. It can be well imagined how this type of total slavery of the individual (i.e. helpless dependence on the state) must be hampering all his chances and hopes to rise higher and evolve himself according to his likings. Thus, it is clear, that both the prevalent systems are one-sided, incomplete and lead to the same problems of exploitation and suppression of the masses in general. In this context, when we look into the *Bharatiya* concept of ownership, we find that here an attempt was made to strike a balance between *vyasti* (the individual) and *samasti* (the society). In this system an individual's initiative and interest are fully guarded and on the other and more important side, the right and ownership of the individual are also not allowed to become a hurdle in the advancement of the social interest.[11]

Another important question is, what should our approach in regard to the distribution of wealth and income be? In this regard, the *Bharatiya* Approach fully recognizes the importance of wealth and income-earning activities in life but it also emphasizes that earning should always be done through legal, proper and moral means (*Dharmena Dhanah*).

This means that wealth should not be acquired through immoral means like theft, robbery, corruption, black marketing, hoarding etc. Wealth must be acquired within the accepted social and ethical thresholds of the society. All in all, we must work towards the formulation of a code of conduct, so that people do not lose the motive and incentive to earn wealth, while at the same time it prevents a degenerative rush for acquiring more and more wealth by any means. Keeping this in mind we have to develop two types of systems for the proper and just distribution of wealth and income in the society: Moral system, and Legal System.[12]

When the ethical, righteous, humanistic and divine feelings are aroused in an individual and corresponding socio-cultural institutions and traditions are developed in order to inspire the individual to dedicate his surplus wealth to the good of the society, it is termed as moral **system of distribution.** In a way it is an effort to bring *mamata se samata* (equality through love). This has been referred to in the *Ishopanishad* as (*Tena Tyaktena Bhunjitha*) 'enjoyment through renunciation'. Our traditions have stressed on the practical implementation of such ideas.

It was given much importance that instead of consuming and enjoying alone, one must share his consumption goods and other possessions with other members of the society, and to implement this in practical life a number of socio-religious institutions were evolved in India. In this regard the institutions of *Ista* (*Yajan*, *Daana*, *Dakshina* etc.) and *Purta* (social welfare activities like construction and dedication of wells, tanks, temples, gardens, inns, place for public distribution of food etc.) made a significant contribution in the distribution of wealth in India's social life. The *Bharatiya* Approach believes that a man should not consume all the goods himself but should share them with other members of the society. *Amrit* and *Vighasa* have been considered the uppermost for a householder in Indian tradition. The remainder of *Yajana* is called *Yajan-shesha* or *Amrita*. It means that everyman should give all his wealth to the society, and thus all should take only that portion of the wealth which is assigned to them by the society from this common pool (i.e. *Yajan*) of the society. *Vighasa* means that a householder should take food only after feeding other dependents. Thus the surplus wealth should be used for the welfare of the society. The motto should be *Dharmaaya dhanah* (wealth for social interest).

In our social order a person is expected to look upon every human being as his brother or sister, nay, as himself, and upon humanity as his family. Our philosophy of life does not preach only to care for one's own bread and butter and to be confined to one's own comforts, but advocates happiness and welfare for all. That is why, an Indian says in his prayer:

Sarve bhavantu sukhinah, sarve santu niraamayaah

(May all be happy; May all be healthy; May all obtain the good things; Let not a single individual be cursed with misery.)

That indeed is the test of how the *Bharatiya* philosophers considered humanity as one and indivisible and strived for the good of it as a whole. It is out of this intense desire to see the human race happy and healthy that all the systems of thought and economic orders have flowed in this country.

In this way, through such means a just and fair distribution of wealth takes place in the society in an easy and natural way and disparity is avoided. The dedication to society of the extra wealth that is left over after fulfilling one's needs is the cornerstone of a moral system of distribution. This is a matter of perspective and we know how change of perspective also brings about a corresponding change in behaviour. If a person thinking of material objects as the *prasada* of God consumes it only after distributing it among as many people as possible, it will be bring the maximum satisfaction. Therefore the Indian sages have commented that a person who seeks to consume exclusively is not moral. As the *Atharvaveda* says,

'Earn through a hundred hands and distribute through a thousand hands.'

If a person does not behave in accordance to moral principles and hoards an extremely excessive amount of material objects only for his exclusive consumption, it then becomes necessary to secure the help of law and sometimes to employ even force. This we call the **legal system of distribution.**

Therefore in the *Mangal*-Development scheme, to reduce the disparities in the distribution of wealth, we must have provisions for both a moral and a legal system of distribution. However, moral methods should always be preferred over the legal methods of distribution.

If we want to make the society free form exploitation and social conflicts, and to provide it with real happiness and peace, the distribution system should be based on seven fundamental principles, viz. love , cooperation, equality, service with dedication, renunciation, purity and force. Thus the best distribution system is one which nourishes the economy, makes it free from exploitation, increases its productivity and provides equal opportunity for living and progress. The basic function of a rational distribution will be growth with and through social justice.

10. Recognition of Family as a Basic Socio-Economic Cultural Unit

The family in India has multiple dimensions-social, cultural, religious, economic etc. It is important to understand the importance of this institution and strengthen it once more. A sense of collective responsibility and sharing each other's grief and happiness is its cornerstone. Therefore the atmosphere of the family should foster the growth of cultural and social values, be filled with love, affection, pleasure, happiness and respect and it should be free form tension and egoism. In Western countries about 30 to 40 per cent of their GDP is spent on social security measures by the government. In India, this social security has been taken care of in a much better way through the institution of the family. In our country, the bringing up of children, the care for the elderly, the sick, and the physically challenged must be taken care of within the family structure, as has been done traditionally in a very good way.

The family in India has been a unit for discharging social responsibilities and the preservation of socio-cultural-religious values and traditions. Hence, we must ensure that the family works for the inculcation, development and propagation of social and ethical values, socio-cultural institutions, customs and traditions in tune with the present time. The family in India has traditionally been producing many objects for the fulfillment of their needs. The work that hotels do in Western countries is done in a much better way within the family in India. In our country there is big set-up of family enterprises. The biggest share of the total national savings in India is the savings of families. In this way the family in India is a strong base of the economy. We have to develop a tradition of purchase and consumption of goods and services for the family in accordance to restrained ethical consumption-pattern. There is a great need in today's world to maintain a proper balance between the income-earning activities and our duties and responsibilities towards the family.

11. Self-Confidence and Moral Leadership

Finally, I would like to emphasize that if we wish to rebuild our society according to the *Mangal* Approach, two things are essential: one is the self-confidence and strong will to progress and second is the moral leadership committed to national interest.

In the context of confidence and strong will I want to cite an illustration. Cancer researches at King's College Hospital in London made a long-term study of 54 breast cancer victims who underwent mastectomies. They reported in *The Lancent*, a British Medical Journal, that seven of ten women with a 'Fighting spirit' were alive ten years later, whereas four of five women 'who felt hopeless' on hearing diagnosis had died. This suggests that we have to build within ourselves enough will and confidence to change ourselves and our destiny by our own efforts and resources.

To achieve the goals of *Mangal*-Development and to evolve and implement the corresponding socio-economic infrastructure, it is imperative to develop a spirit of moral and social responsibility in the society at large leading to moral leadership. Only by creating an awareness of self respect and self-reliance through the medium of moral leadership can we move in the direction of *Mangal*-Development. The well-known thinker and Nobel Laureate Prof. Gunar Myrdal had said that the solution to India's problems is not foreign loan and foreign investment, but rather moral leadership. In this regard Prof. Myrdal seems completely correct when he says:

".......often, when labouring with India's staggering development problems, I have felt inclined to believe that what that great country needs today, more than foreign aid and day-to-day adjustments of policies to meet the recurring emergencies, is spiritual leaders approaching Gandhiji's greatness, his love and fearlessness. Together with all the patriots who would undoubtedly come to surround such leaders, they might electrify the nation to undertake the

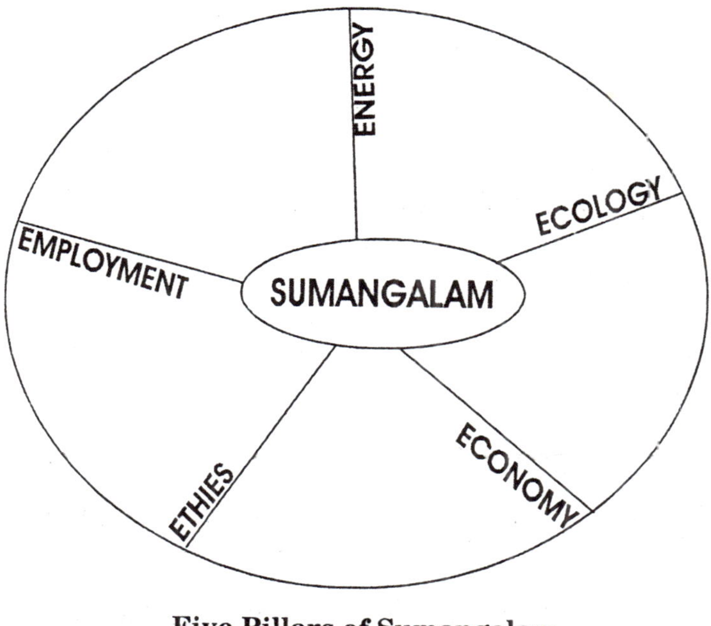

Five Pillars of Sumangalam

revolutionary changes in social, economic and political institutions, aptitudes and practices which are now so desperately needed."[13]

To sum up, we can say that in *Mangal*-Development we will set up such a structure in which there will be a balance between ethics, economy, ecology, energy and employment.

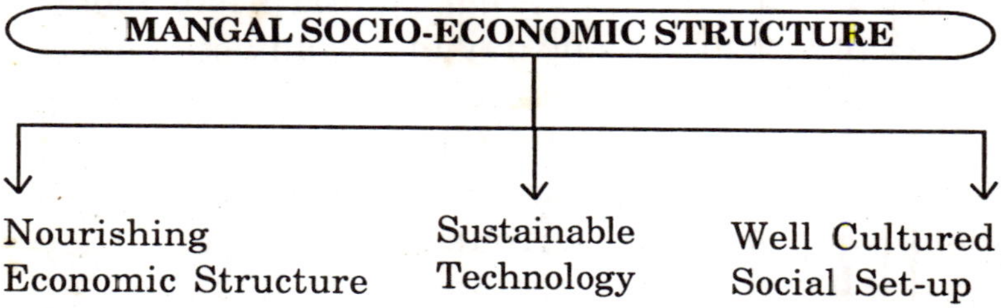

It we could really maintain a good synthesis and proper integration among these five elements it will give birth to a new kind of socio- economic structure. This new socio-economic structure will be based on three following interrelated domentions

1. Nourishing Economic Structure

2. Sustainable Technology

3. Well cultured social set-up (Sanskaarksham Samaajtantra)

References

1. United Nations Industrial Development Organisation, Delhi Meet, 1978.

2. Kalam, APJ Abdul with Rajan, Y.S.; India 2020-A Vision for the New Millennium, 1998, p. 139.

3. Murdivallabhan, TV; Dimensions of Sustainable Economic Developement, 2005, pp. 26, 57.

4. Mahapragya, Acharya and Kalam, APJ Abdul; The family and the Nation, 2008, p. 181.

5. Mahabharat, Shantiparva, 8, pp. 77-80.

6. Shyamacharan (Dr.), Dubey; Vikas ka Samajshastra, Vaani Prakashan, N. Delhi, 1996, p. 87.

7. Joshi, M.M.; Science Sustainability and Indian National Resurgence, 2008, pp. 57, 77, 80, 84.

8. Mahapragya and Kalam; op. cit., p. 25.

9. Mahapragya and Kalam; op. cit., p. 11.

10. Mahapragya and Kalam; op. cit, p. 26.

11. Gupta, B.L.; Value and Distribution System in Ancient India, 1992, p. 260.

12. For detail discussion see, Gupta, B.L.; op. cit., pp. 264-287.

13. Myrdal, Gunnar; Against the stream, p. 244.

Index

N

O

P